HAUNTED

NEATH

The view over Neath.

HAUNTED

NEATH

ROBERT KING

Dedication

This book is dedicated to my late uncle, Edward John King of Rectory Road, Neath, who nurtured my interest in:

Goldies and ghosties
And long legged beasties
And things that go
Bump in the night.

(A Cornish legend)

First published 2009

The History Press
The Mill, Brimscombe Port
Stroud, Gloucestershire, GL5 2QG
www.thehistorypress.co.uk

ISBN 978 0 7524 5005 6

Typesetting and origination by The History Press
Printed in Great Britain

CONTENTS

Acknowledgements   7

Foreword   9

1   Street Hauntings   11

2   Property Hauntings   17

3   Neath Abbey   29

4   Public Houses   35

5   Llantwit Cemetery   51

6   Poltergeists   55

7   Outside the Town   61

8   Miscellaneous Hauntings   79

ACKNOWLEDGEMENTS

I have been interested in the paranormal for many years and am indebted to the following for helping me collect the experiences published in this book: the late Miss Gertie Bowen; the late Mike Richards of the Dark Arch public house; the late John Blackmore; Mr Peter Rees of the Star Inn, Penydre; the late Mrs Margaret Jones; Mr Peter Williams; Mr John Jones; Mrs Pat Ellis; Mr Phil Thomas; Maggie King; Mr Brady; Peter Healey and Barry Flint.

I'm particularly grateful to Mr James Rees of the Castle Hotel, Neath for all his help; to Mike Davies for taking the photographs; to Paul Davies for correcting my PC glitches, and to my wife Joy for her tolerance about my ghost hunting jaunts ('Don't bring them home with you'), as well as her enthusiasm and constant encouragement.

FOREWORD

Neath has had a rich and varied history since the Roman Invasion. The town was certainly in existence from AD 70 when the Romans developed Nidum to suppress the angry Silures, building a fort on the western side of the River Neath. The Romans also built Coelbren Fort, as well as a huge marching camp on Heol Morfydd above Tonna called Blaen Cwm Bach. Imagine the galleons navigating the river to the point we now call Roman Way; there was no canal, road or railway then for unloading the vast amount of material for the development and subsequent maintenance of these forts.

After the Romans left Briton around AD 410 we entered the 'Age of the Saints' (called the Dark Ages in English history) and the further development of Christianity. The Welsh Princes resisted every move by their cousins and brothers, and became even more aggressive when Britain was invaded by the Normans, who created the borough system. They built a castle as the Romans before them had built a fort; the Welsh were a difficult people to suppress and those who lived in this part of the country were as determined not to be trespassed upon as anyone.

The development of the town from the twelfth century saw the building of the monastery at Neath Abbey, which saw several royal visits through the centuries. The town played an important part in the burgeoning industrial development of the late Middle Ages; the Mines Royal Copper Company was started in Aberdulais in the sixteenth century, and the coming of Sir Humphrey Mackworth to the

Gnoll spearheaded the production of mineral wealth that was to be the hallmark of the town.

The changes have been huge. Indeed in recent years, areas of the town bear no resemblance to what they were even forty or fifty years ago. Redevelopment has swept away hovels and roads that once housed the life-blood of our forefathers.

This turbulent past, and the changes that have occurred, give us a rich source of material for unexplainable happenings, spooky stories and frightening occurrences that have certainly upset and shocked people. I have been collecting such tales for many years, and have spoken to many people, men and women, who you would think would be the very last to believe in ghostly happenings. But they remain steadfast in that belief.

I merely record these stories. In the following pages some names have been altered to protect the individuals, but others are quite forthright about what they believe they have seen or felt, and are willing to have their names recorded.

Robert King
Abergarwed 2009

One

STREET HAUNTINGS

The Victorian Policeman

Gerald Rhys Thomas from the Cimla was walking along Penydre late on a Friday night in January 1962. The sky was clear as he hurried home after leaving his girlfriend, Sarah, safely at her home near the Star Inn. His thoughts were concentrated on his romance and the marriage that was planned for March that year. Ever practical, the couple were marrying before the end of the tax year to enable them to reclaim a year's paid tax.

He passed the dark, forbidding Mission Hall and turned into Old Market Street. The town clock chimed out two o'clock. The street was absolutely empty. His hard-soled shoes echoed gently against the buildings, the moon danced above the roofs of the shops as he crossed Navvies' Square into Water Street. 'I'll be home in twenty minutes', he remembers thinking.

The many public houses in this part of Neath had long thrown out their last customers, cleaned and locked up. He could still smell the aroma of stale beer, as he dodged a pool of vomit outside the Shakespeare. He heard the sound of a door being shaken.

He felt in his pocket for one of his Woodbine cigarettes and rolled it in his lips to moisten it. From the doorway of the pub appeared a policeman, dressed in a cape that hung from his neck to just above his waist.

Rugby Avenue.

Gerald paused, expecting the policeman to ask him where he was going. Anyone out late during that time could expect to be asked what they were doing and where they were going. The policeman looked at him and nodded with a faint smile.

'Hello, officer,' said Gerald, remembering to be deliberately affable. Provoke a policeman late at night during those years and you could find yourself under arrest. 'Quiet night?' The policeman cleared the phlegm from his throat but didn't answer. '…Been to my girlfriend's house,' Gerald offered. The town clock sounded quarter past two.

The policeman remained silent as he stepped off the kerb and crossed the road. Gerald started to walk on. He heard the door of Bush's Sport Shop being tried with a loud rattle as he felt in his pocket for a match. He couldn't find any, 'Must have left them at Sarah's', he thought.

The chip shop next to Bush's felt the force of the hand of the law, as he tested for forgetful shopkeepers. Gerald turned to ask the policeman if he had a match, but although the chip shop door was being rattled, there was no sign of the copper.

He was frozen to the spot. He wished he was either in his own home or that of Sarah's. The door stopped rattling. Gerald started to run but before he had moved ten yards, the policeman appeared in front of him, trying another doorway.

'I missed you,' said Gerald, almost relieved to see him, but he couldn't understand why he had disappeared from sight. The amber street light glanced across the policeman's cape, 'I was going to ask you if you have got a match?'

It only then occurred to Gerald that the clothes worn by policeman didn't conform to that used by modern officers. He felt himself begin to tremble. 'H-have you g-got a m-match?'

The policeman walked on without answering and walked straight through the wall of the next shop.

Gerald stared at what he had seen. The threads of tobacco of the unlit cigarette tasted bitter in his mouth. He spat them out. Suddenly the policeman appeared from the exact same spot in the wall, but this time accompanied by two others. They moved purposefully towards him and shouted, 'Stop, police!'. The shrill sound of their whistles filled the echoing street.

Gerald, terrified, walked backward and stumbled against the kerb. He stepped in a pool of vomit but managed to regain his balance. The three policemen menacingly came closer. One had a handlebar moustache.

'Police!' the shout went up again. Gerald turned and ran back the way he'd come from, towards Sarah's home. He glanced back only once, and he thought he saw a faint glow at the crossroads of Navvies' Square, but absolutely breathless he continued running until he was hammering on Sarah's front door, shouting for them to get up and let him in.

Rugby Avenue

A pleasant tree-lined avenue on the edge of the centre of town, behind Victoria Gardens, the houses in Ena Avenue are late Victorian and early Edwardian. This strange haunting was told to me in the early 1960s by Maurice Wiltshire, who was then in his late eighties.

He said that between the wars, about 1925, he was walking home from town late one August afternoon:

I was not hurrying… I was making my way from Penydre to Stockham's Corner.
I often went through Ena Avenue and then Rugby Avenue and out into Bilton Road
and along Eastland Road to the bottom of Windsor Road.

Old Market Street looking towards Navvies' Square amd Water Street.

I was smoking and thinking of nothing in particular when a stick hit me on the head. It hurt too. I cursed and looked around rubbing my head. I wasn't happy. 'What the 'ell,' I said out loud, picking up the stick, one that probably had fallen into the gutter in the winter. But the road was empty, save for the trees.

I thought that some kid was messing about and hiding from me. I moved to the centre of the road and continued walking. All I saw was a shadow, but suddenly it moved, trying to hide from me behind one of the trees.

'Right you, come here,' I shouted, running to the tree. As I ran a small stone hit me on the shoulder, which was followed by laughter.

When I got to the tree, which only took a few seconds as I could run a bit in those days, there was nothing there. I stood perplexed. Then across the road a child, about seven or eight years old, dressed much as we all did in those days – a flat cap with the pronounced peak, shirt open to the neck covering the neckerchief, ragged trousers, a rough jacket and heavy boots. There must be two of them, I thought.

'Come here, you,' I shouted and ran towards him.

Again there was nothing. I felt around the tree with my arms because I hadn't seen him run off. But… nothing. I just waited a few minutes and walked on a few steps. Something made me turn around quickly and standing near one of the trees was the child. I stared at him. He laughed and slowly, so slowly and still smiling, disappeared before my eyes. I blinked and rubbed my eyes. What had I seen? A ghost? But remember, this was in the afternoon, an August afternoon with the sun shining brightly. And there was no one about.

I was a little frightened but pulled myself together. I walked on still in the middle of the road and just before I came to Bilton Road I heard the laughter again. I tuned around but the road was empty.

Maurice said that he had often mused about the incident. 'I know what I saw,' he said. 'I know, too, what I felt when that stick and then the stone hit me. I did walk the road again, many times but nothing like that ever happened to me again.'

He laughed at the recollection.

Two

PROPERTY HAUNTINGS

The Man in the Window

In 1966 Phil Thomas was eighteen years old and working for a firm of local builders based in the town. He usually walked to work through Victoria Gardens, past the Cross Keys public house and along Water Street to his firm's base. He'd followed this route for months that year.

One morning he was hurrying past the houses at the top of the street and heard a knocking on an upstairs window. Pausing, he turned and saw an old gentleman waving to him. The window was slightly open and the man said, 'Good morning'.

Phil didn't know him but out of courtesy waved back and said, 'Yes, thanks' as he hurried on. Later that afternoon, Phil's boss said that they were calling in to a property at the top end of Water Street. He had a contract to renovate it. Phil was amazed when they entered the same house from where he had been acknowledged by the old man. What he saw inside the house was absolute dereliction. The house hadn't been occupied for some months and had been securely locked. As far as his boss was concerned, no one could have accessed the place.

Phil thought no more about it until forty-three years later. Now he was sixty-one years of age and retired from work. He had started the fascinating subject of studying family history. Researching back through his maternal line, he was totally

Water Street.

flabbergasted to learn that his mother's father, his grandfather, had been born and had lived in the same house.

He had never met him. What did Phil see that morning in 1966 when he was eighteen years of age?

The Gnoll House

The first reference to the Gnoll House was in 1632 when the High Sheriff of Glamorgan, David Evans, was recorded as living there.

The name associated with the Gnoll that posterity remembers is that of Mackworth. It started in 1680 when Sir Humphrey Mackworth, the Member of Parliament for Cardiganshire, married Anne Evans, thus becoming the owner of the house. The family would dominate the Gnoll for the next 114 years.

The Gnoll House.

Mackworth was a prodigious industrialist and most documents and educational television programmes that deal with the development of industrial Britain include him as being in the top five early entrepreneurs who were prepared to gamble their money by investing in the copper, iron and coal trades.

He was a religious man and actually made provisions for the children of his employees to be educated. He was also one of the first Parliamentarians to advocate that free libraries should be established with funding from the state. This caused much hilarity in Parliamentary circles, not that such mocking behaviour would have caused him any distress.

The Mackworth era ended when Sir Robert Mackworth died in 1794. His widow, Molly, remarried and left the town. In 1811 the estate was purchased by Henry Grant. His son, Henry John Grant, became the first Mayor of Neath in 1836. Following Henry John's death, the estate passed on to his nephew Charles Evan Thomas. It was from this family that Neath Borough Council bought the estate in 1923.

The only ghost story associated with the Gnoll that I have heard is the one relating to Henry Grant, who purchased the estate in 1811, and who died in 1831. Following his death, and until recent times, a lady dressed in white has been seen hurrying about the precincts of where the house once stood, calling out in the middle of the night, 'Henry, Henry!'

Presumably this is Mrs Grant. I don't doubt that the suddenness of her presence has cooled the ardour of many courting couples who used the Gnoll as a lovers' lane.

The Dancing Blue Light

Until her death three years ago at the age of eighty-seven, Mrs Whiteham had lived in Rhydhir in Neath Abbey since the estate had been built in the late 1940s. She had been born in the Dulais Valley and carried a very distinctive mark on the left-hand side of her face.

This mark was the size of a pound coin and had caused concern to both herself and her mother since the day she had been born. Her mother had taken her to see

Rhydhir on the Longford Estate.

several doctors and plastic surgeons, naturally the object being to have it removed. Doctors, though, had said to leave it, 'We don't know what will happen if we start tampering with it. It is deep seated,' had been the consensus.

'I will get rid of that one day,' her mother had always said.

By 1955 Mrs Whiteham had married, was living in Rhydhir, Longford and she had three children. She was now aged forty-one. Her mother had died suddenly that November; she had been ill for only a matter of weeks.

The news of her mother's death arrived following a visit by her brother-in-law at 6p.m. in the evening, as there weren't many telephones around then. 'Mam' had passed away at 3p.m. that afternoon After the brother-in-law had moved on to the next relative, Mrs Whiteham stood alone by the bedroom window reflecting on her mother. Whenever she was nervous or worried she rubbed her fingers on the mark on her cheek.

She told me the following story some years ago:

I dropped off to sleep just after midnight. My husband was already fast asleep, he had to be up at five to get ready to go to work in the colliery.

It must have been about three o'clock when I was disturbed. There was a blue light, only small at first; it seemed to be just hanging in the corner of the room, near the ceiling. I just stared at it, terrified. Unable to move. There wasn't a sound. And then it moved and got bigger, emitting a deeper blue light until the entire room was enveloped in it. I roused my husband and he too was both frightened and amazed.

'What it is?' he whispered.

Before I could answer the light seemed to suddenly darken and grew smaller until it was about the size of a football, then it reduced still further to the size of a tennis ball and hovered above the bed. My husband and I were holding each others hands under the bedclothes, unable to move with fear.

Then the blue light move slowly to the window and just passed through the glass and literally disappeared from our sight. We lay there for what seemed ages, pretty shocked at what we both had seen. My husband couldn't settle afterwards and we both looked in on the children, who were all fast asleep, before going downstairs to make a cup of tea.

We sat downstairs until it was time for him to go to work. It was still too early to wake the children, two of whom were of school age. I just sat there on my own thinking about the light and wondering what it could have been.

I was glad when seven o'clock came because now I could rouse the children in readiness for school. I went back upstairs to the bathroom to wash and freshen up and when I looked in the mirror, the brown mole had noticeably faded. I couldn't understand it. There was no itching on my skin, it hadn't been touched, yet it was virtually only a slight blemish.

The children didn't notice and I was happy when they had gone to school. I saw to the baby, and asked my next door neighbour whether there had been any lightning in the night?

I was assured that there hadn't been.

Later that day my sister called; she had lived with my mother, and said that the funeral arrangements were being made. Then she asked, 'What's the matter with your face?'

I touched the place where the blemish had been. The skin was smooth, the mark had gone.

'Where's the mark?' she asked.

I told her about the blue light and how during the course of the last few hours the mark had disappeared. Like me, she was shocked.

When my husband came home from work he, too, was amazed.

The following day I went to see Doctor Roberts at his surgery in the Ropewalk in Neath. He had been our family doctor for many years. He condoled with me about my mother as he gently ran his fingers over my cheek and shook his head.

'I can't explain it,' he said. 'A blue light you said?'

'Yes, it was frightening and lasted about ten minutes.'

'There's no explanation that I can offer,' he said sitting down, removing his glasses and looking at my face.

And there never was an explanation for the mark's disappearance. Did Mrs Whiteham's mother fulfil her promise? 'I'll get rid of that one day' she always said. So did she take it with her as she moved to the afterlife?

The Rocking Chair

Science tells us that there is no such thing as perpetual motion. Nothing can continue to move without some form of aid. A worrying fact if you consider that one day even the Earth will stop spinning. Such facts were far from Debra and David Russell's minds the day they were told that they had inherited her grandmother's house on Gnoll Park Road.

Newly married and living with Debra's parents in the Cimla, they eagerly anticipated their move into the spacious, four bedroom semi-detached house

Gnoll Park Road.

located in a much sought after part of the town. The legacy dimmed the grief they felt about Gran's passing. They couldn't even afford to buy a flat, let alone such a large house. They understandably felt lucky.

The family allowed the couple to start clearing the house of its old furniture and start the preparations to redecorate the rooms. Everything was cleared with the exception of a rocking chair and some pictures that were in the downstairs front room of the house.

'Gran liked that chair, we'll keep that,' Debra had told David. 'But get rid of those old pictures. No one wants them, I've asked. Dump them in the skip.' David agreed. The pictures depicted long-forgotten relatives sitting in groups, their stern faces and immaculate Victorian and Edwardian clothes dominating the scenes that were being recorded.

The furniture and carpets from every room had been removed. The wallpaper had been stripped and most of the old paint burned away in readiness for the redecorating. David had even started clearing the back garden. The couple's enthusiasm and happiness was boundless.

But it was all to go so terribly wrong for them as Debra and David told me one evening when I met them in the Queen's public house on Victoria Gardens, now renamed the Canterbury:

I had taken tins of paint and everything I needed to redecorate and had piled them all in the hallway. Some time earlier I had taken the only remaining item of Gran's furniture and put it in the kitchen out of the way.

When I tried to open the door it seemed jammed, but by pushing I managed to get it open enough to squeeze in. What had been obstructing the door was the rocking chair.

I thought maybe Debra's father had popped down and had left it there and somehow it had jammed the door. But he said he hadn't been near the house since I had taken the paint there. I moved the chair back into the kitchen and started the redecorating work.

I had finished the picture rail, Deb's and I had liked that, and although it is old fashioned we decided to keep it, and had started on the skirting boards when I heard a bang coming from the kitchen. I went into the hall and I could see the rocking chair where I had put it, but now it was gently rocking to and fro.

I admit I was scared. I had never seen anything like it. I tentatively walked towards it and then went put my foot against the chair and suddenly it increased its rocking speed. I backed away, grabbed my coat and went home.

I was disturbed but said nothing about this to anyone. The more I thought about it, the more I became convinced that it had been my imagination. Nevertheless, when Deb's dad suggested I take some more things to the house I asked him to come with me. He couldn't so I made some excuse and would do it the day after.

A couple of days passed before Debra, her father and I filled the boot of the car with various items and drove to the house. I had still said nothing about what I had seen.

Deb's father was naturally thrilled that we had been bequeathed the house and was telling us stories as we went down Cimla Hill about his courting days in the house.

He was telling us that he wasn't allowed in the front room with Deb's mother unless the door was open. But he had got on well with her parents and used to go to the Gnoll to watch the All Blacks playing. The ground is just across the road, of course.

Through all this light-hearted chat I was dreading going into the house. But I did hope that it had been my imagination and that I had been stupid.

Dad went in first and complimented me on the little painting I had completed. Debra immediately asked me why I hadn't moved the rocking chair out of the room before starting the decorating.

'I did,' I answered.

'You put it back then?' she said.

Suddenly I got stuck for words. I didn't want to tell her about the rocking chair. But when I had last left the house it had been still in the kitchen. Now it was in what Gran had used as a living room—this is the room I had been painting. I looked. There is was, facing the empty fireplace.

'I'll leave you two and pop into town,' said Deb's father, 'I'll be back in an hour.'

Deb's kissed him on the check and said all right. The door closed behind him and we started to sort out some things we had brought down. There was still more in the car. Debra said lets walk about the house, see each room again. Make plans. She still couldn't believe how lucky we were. I agreed and we went upstairs and stared at the spacious bedrooms. We had already decided which one was going to be 'ours'. We could hear a few sparrows chirping in the attic and said that we would have to sort out the outside of the house. At that moment everything was really serene and peaceful and I did begin to relax.

David and Debra paused in the telling of the story and Debra tearfully said that as they walked back down the stair they could hear the gentle rocking sound of the chair coming from Gran's living room. Debra said, 'I didn't know what it was, of course, but David did and he was white. I asked, "What's that?" I soon found out because the chair was moving back and fro just like it had always done when Gran had been there'.

Debra said that they were both rooted to the spot, while the chair kept on moving. 'I started to cry and David held me tight. I asked him what was happening'.

The couple explained that they realised there was some form of supernatural phenomena in progress but that it was completely beyond their comprehension. They did, though, know instinctively that it was Debra's grandmother.

'What are we going to do?' Debra asked David.

'Don't know. Your dad won't be long. Let's wait here.'

They waited. And as they did the faint outline of a lady began to appear before their eyes. Gradually, it became more focused until one would not have known that the presence wasn't flesh and blood.

In a state of panic Debra rushed for the door screaming. David turned to look into the room before he followed her. When he looked, the chair was empty and not moving.

They ran out of the house holding hands and met Debra's father near the old Civic Centre and between the incoherent descriptions they all headed back to the house. Debra's father was sceptical and asked them if they had been drinking.

'You'll see, you'll see,' Debra said almost hysterically.

But when they arrived back at the house all was calm. The chair was still there but completely still.

The couple's insistence prevailed and to try and placate them, Debra's father said he would get rid of the rocking chair.

The couple agreed but were still in a state of shock. As they watched her father go to the chair and pick it up, saying, 'This will sort out your daft problem,' the chair seemed to be grabbed from him and was thrown against the wall. It clattered down and lay still. He walked backwards to the door and turned to the couple and said, 'Let's get out.'

What had appeared to be an ideal start to the newlyweds married life had turned into a nightmare. No one could explain why. If the grandmother hadn't wanted them to have the house why had she bequeathed it to them? Debra had spent many hours in the house with both her grandparents and more time since her granddad had died. She had got on very well with her gran. So why should she return to haunt them in such a spectacular and frightening way?

They never did live in the house. The rocking chair was burned; the house was sold and was turned into a home for older people.

David reflected that whenever he passes along Gnoll Park Road he always glances at the house. 'What was it all about? I had never thought about ghosts or anything like that but three of us saw Gran. And why was the chair, which was heavy yet went across the room as though it was piece of firewood, snatched from Deb's father and smashed against the wall?' He shook his head in wonderment.

The Workman

A Neath priest related to me how he responded to a call for help from a lady living in a block of flats on Victoria Gardens. The lady, who was well into her seventies, had seen the bizarre sight of a man wheeling a barrow through her living room and disappearing through the wall. This was happening a few times a week. She was understandably distressed.

The reverend gentleman explained that the ghost never looked at the lady, never uttered a word, made no noise whatsoever, but merely passed by as though the dwelling wasn't there.

The usual rites were carried out with copious quantities of holy water sprinkled. He hoped that the spirit was laid. He left crucifixes in several locations in the flat.

A few days later his phone rang, and the lady told him that the spirit was still there.

Victoria Gardens. The public library is on the far right.

The ritual was carried out again. She told the priest that the ghost was taking no notice of the religious rites. But it clearly wasn't offended, because would he not have been annoyed at them for trying to get rid of him?

This perplexed the priest because it seemed to him that the lady wasn't so distressed by the haunting as she had seemed only a few days ago, and he made another visit. He told me that one doesn't doubt such reports, one tries to deal with them, but nevertheless he was getting sceptical about it.

The road outside was, as usual, very busy when he rang the specific number on the bell and locking panel. It wasn't answered. With that the communal door was opened and a man came out, so he took the opportunity of going in. This time he rang the door and knocked. No answer. He knocked a neighbour's door who told him that she hadn't been seen since the day before. But the neighbour knew a key holder who lived nearby.

Once entry had been gained, the key holder and the priest found the lady dead in her bed, seemingly peaceful, a smile locked by death on her face.

The ambulance was called and the police, which is normal with instances of sudden death. After the body had been removed something caught the reverend's eye as he left the flat. The movement was brief, but the wheelbarrow creaked as it went through the wall.

As far as he knows, no workman with a barrow has been seen in the flats since.

Three

NEATH ABBEY

Among the oldest buildings in Neath, and arguably the most iconic, are the ruins of the Church of St Mary, Neath Abbey. In 1539 Thomas Cromwell, the Vicar General in the employ of King Henry VIII removed the monks, stripped the roof and allowed the weather in. Nature did the rest. Those souls that haunt the Abbey naturally pre-date this, from 1129 when the charter was granted to the House of Savigny to establish a monastery on the banks of the Nedd. The house of Savegny collapsed a few years later and it joined with the Cistercian Order. Their ghosts continue to frequent the still and now jagged walls to the present day.

In 1326 King Edward II took refuge in the Abbey. He was in fear of his life being perused by his enemies, among whom were his wife and her lover, who aspired to kill him and seize the seals of state.

At that time all monastic buildings were a refuge from the law, so the King's enemies had to wait and watch until he decided to try and escape. For some ten days he was looked after by the monks until he made his escape.

The story goes that one of the brothers (or a lay brother) had conspired with Isabella and Robert Mortimer and passed information to them about the route the King would take on leaving the Abbey. The information proved correct and King Edward was captured, taken to Berkeley Castle and executed. Upon hearing this the abbot and his brethren were no doubt distressed. That distress turned to anger when they learned that one of their own number had divulged the route.

Remains of the Abbot's House, Neath Abbey. It later became a Tudor mansion.

A view of the lay brothers' quarters, Neath Abbey.

Was that person killed and his body not buried in consecrated ground? Many people claim to have seen a figure dressed in a habit of the Cistercian Order. He always has a sad, if not desperate, expression on his face. Is he wandering for eternity seeking forgiveness?

The Genial Monk

The ruin of the western gatehouse is still to be seen next to Neath Abbey Infants School. It is through this gate that the monks would have left to make their way to Cwrt–y–Clafdy, the monastery's infirmary.

You have to imagine the route that they would have taken; the system of roads and tracks would have been completely different to those we see today. The monks would probably have created a walk that took them through what is now St John's churchyard across the land that occupies the railway, up what is now Hill Road and on to the infirmary.

A few years ago I gave a talk to the Neath branch of the U3A (University of the Third Age). After the lecture members ask questions and then we all have tea. A gentleman came up to me and said, 'We see them, you know'. He was aged, in his seventies, and as it transpired was a retired engineer.

'See whom?' I asked.

'The monks,' he said.

His wife came up to us, 'You've told him, then?' He nodded.

I realised that they were both well educated and not given to fanciful thoughts or ideas. They clearly had seen something.

'What do you mean exactly?' I asked.

The gentleman continued, 'In your talk you described the route you thought they would take on the way to the hospital. Well that would take them right through our house. And we have seen them walking through. They all look solid, just like real people save for their clothes and the fact that they walk through the wall and disappear. The clothes are typical of those worn by monks. They are monks.'

'How many times have you seen them?' I asked.

'Many times,' he said.

'When was the last time?' I asked.

'A few months ago. It doesn't bother us anymore.'

His wife confirmed this and said, 'They know we are there, too'. The gentleman continued:

A few years ago we had our first computer and it was in the living room. Now this room is not on the route that they take. You have to see them to know that they are there. They make absolutely no noise. It was about two o'clock in the morning and I was working on the computer with the all the lights in the house switched off. I suddenly became aware that someone or something was behind me. I was frightened and tried to look around, only slowly moving my head. Then I saw him. A genial face, his white robes up to his neck. I moved my head further around and I saw him clearly. He was looking over my shoulder at the computer. Then our eyes met and he smiled. I was too stunned to smile back. And then, so suddenly, he disappeared. I was shaken, I put the lights on and turned off the computer and hurried to bed.

Hill Road, Neath Abbey. This is a possible route the monks could have used to reach the infirmary.

Procession

The same couple who have seen the ghosts of monks in their house, not far from Hill Road, also told me that on occasions they process through in Indian file, looking straight ahead and that there are so many in the procession that it sometimes takes a full five minutes for them to disappear through the wall and out of the house. One strange thing is that they are never seen walking in the direction of the Abbey, only going towards the infirmary.

Another couple, residents of Hill Road for more than thirty years, have also told me that they have seen 'strange apparition-type whispery shapes' making their way, again in Indian file, up the hill leading to Drummau Road and then presumably towards Cwrt-y-Clafdy.

Another link with the Hill Road area was a story told me by the late Mrs Margaret Thomas:

> There is a photograph that was taken during the early 1950s when grandchildren visiting their grandparents, who lived on Hill Road, were taken on a visit to the Abbey's ruins on a summer evening.
>
> Like most people the children loved the place and after running about there and listening to their grandfather talking about the history of the place, the children were lined up to be photographed.
>
> Some weeks later when the pictures had been developed they showed a lovely image of the children but posing behind them was the figure, clearly seen, of a monk dressed in the traditional garments of the Cistercian Order.

Mrs Thomas had seen this picture and said the negative had been sent to Kodak for analysis, for examination, to see if it had been tampered with. Kodak could offer no technical explanation in respect of the ghostly image. I haven't seen this picture but don't doubt that it exists.

four

PUBLIC HOUSES

The Castle Hotel

The most prominent hostelry in the town, and one of the oldest, is the Castle Hotel. Dominating the parade with an air of well-kept elegance, it is the place where most of the visiting celebrities and VIPs will stay. At various periods in its history it has been known as the Ship and Castle Inn, the Castle Inn and now, of course, the Castle Hotel. It is also arguably the town's most haunted building.

Early records tell us that it was built in 1695, but was unnamed and traded under the landlord's name, which was 'Proffs'. It has been the focus for many events, important meetings and seminars. In 1699 Sir Edward Mansel dined there after visiting the Melyncrythan Works; in 1784 the Gnoll Masonic Lodge 'removed to the Ship and Castle Inn', as the landlord then was William Meyrick, himself a mason; in 1786 Charles Nott, the father of Major General Sir William Nott who was in charge of the defence of Candahar in 1842, became its landlord. Sir William Nott's birth date coincides with his father's tenure of the inn. Charles Nott left Neath in 1796 for the Ivy Bush in Carmarthen. In 1796 Lewis Roterley took over the management of the inn but after only four years he left for the Mackworth Arms in Swansea. Like his predecessor he had a prominent son, Major Lewis Roterley, who was Lieutenant of Marines on the *Cleopatra* at Martinique in 1808.

The Castle Hotel.

From 1789 the trustees of the Neath Turnpike Trust held their meetings at the inn, and the auction for the letting of the toll gates was held there. From 1792 until 1808 it was the venue of the committee briefed with the rebuilding of the Neath River Bridge; Lord Nelson and Lady Hamilton are said to have frequented the inn on a number of occasions; and in more recent times Richard Burton and Elizabeth Taylor were guests. In addition it was in the Nelson Room in 1881 that the Welsh Rugby Union was formed.

In about 1845 a wager was made at the Castle Hotel by Captain Frederick Fredericks of Dyffryn that he could fire a revolver through a mirror without breaking it except for the hole the bullet would make. This wager was won by the Captain and the mirror was a feature in the Nelson Bar until it was lost some years ago during a refurbishment.

The Castle was the principal stop and change over for the Mail Coach travelling from London to Milford; coaches also left bound for Swansea, Merthyr, Brecon and Gloucester. The large area used as coach houses and stabling was behind the Parade, now used as a car park and an array of small businesses. The sound of horses' shod hooves on the cobbled yards and the clanging of blacksmiths' hammers would have been a constant sound.

The current proprietor, Mr James Rees, has recorded several strange happenings following discussion with Mr Darrel Jeremiah, a former general manager of the Castle Hotel.

The Chambermaid

Sometime in 1845 a chambermaid hanged herself from a ceiling rose in the hotel's old wing. In 2003 an investigation was carried out in the hotel by Mr Gifford's Psychic Fare, and a medium revealed that the young girl was about seventeen years of age and working in the service of the Bloods of Neath, who owned the business at that time. The psychic described an image of the girl leaning out of the window that backed on to what is now New Street, looking at her lover who is on horseback, dressed in hunting pink. She is heavily pregnant with his child.

Convention in society at that time dictated that it wasn't acceptable for a gentleman of her lover's status to marry the lowly bred chambermaid, expecting a child or not. Thus, considering her condition she was desperate and her mind would have been in turmoil.

The lover rode off to enjoy his day's hunting, leaving her behind and possibly unaware, but I doubt that, of her emotional state. Had she accepted that their love or any concern for the unborn child could entice the huntsman to marry her? Faced with the prospect of bringing up a child out of wedlock and fearing the

The Castle Hotel from New Street.

The corridor outside rooms 14 and 15 where the ghost of a young girl has been seen.

scorn with which she would be treated, she hanged herself from the ceiling and slowly strangled.

This poor girl has been seen leaning out of the window in a distressed state, probably pleading with the horseman to have consideration for her.

It wasn't known to the medium that the stable yard being described is now the back of the shops on New Street.

The Old Ball Room

Following a paranormal research investigation in 2005, the presence of an old man and several orbs were detected in this room. Through the medium the old man revealed that he was a stable hand. The Old Ball Room was built over the hotel's old stable block. This information was not known to the investigation team at that time.

Room 16

This room is said to be haunted by a woman who burnt to death there some time during the early 1800s. Members of the hotel's housekeeping staff have fled screaming from the room after hearing loud thudding noises. A previous housekeeper said that if the staff rearranged items of furniture in the room, the ghost of the woman would become angry and cause objects to move suddenly.

Rooms 14 & 15

In the corridor outside rooms 14 and 15, a young girl has been seen on various occasions, apparently floating up into the wall. Following the examination of a set of old structural plans of the hotel, it was discovered that at the point where the girl was seen there was once a staircase leading up to the servants' quarters.

Upon investigation of these hidden rooms, it was found that they had been gutted by fire, possibly the fire that cut through the building in the 1800s. It appears that a decision was made to seal up these servants' rooms and remove the staircase. Could it be the haunting of the chambermaid who tragically hanged herself and is making her way to the safety of her room?

The Lady in a White Robe

Over the years many members of staff have reported seeing a red-haired woman, dressed in a flowing white robe (or is it a shroud?) in the corridor outside rooms 25 and 26.

The front entrance of the hotel where the Lady in Black has been seen.

Little is known about her, although her presence has always left those members of staff who have seen her feeling uneasy and saddened rather that frightened.

Room 4

This room is now used as a guests' room but was once, many years ago, used as a residence by the then owners of the business. This room does seem to have uneasiness about it. Those who have experienced it say that objects have been known to fall from shelves and shatter for no apparent reason. Two residents who had been booked into this room reported to the manager the following morning the various disturbances that they had experienced.

They both felt a weight at the bottom of the bed reminiscent of someone sitting on the end of it. They did fall asleep, only to be woken up by a banging noise that

The main stairwell frequented by the Lady in Black.

came from somewhere in the room, but strangely they couldn't pinpoint exactly where. 'It seemed to be everywhere, all around us,' they reported, 'but it lasted throughout the night'. Not surprisingly they requested to be allocated another room for the duration of their stay in Neath.

Christmas Eve Haunting
Christmas Eve is one of the most evocative nights in the calendar and on this date in 1998, the deputy manager and one member of the staff were sitting in the foyer. All the guests had left and the hotel was closed, and all the lights were off save for the one in the foyer. Christmas Day then was a rare day off. The hotel had been checked to make sure that no one was on the premises. The building was empty and the heavy silence that fills such usually busy buildings had settled over the area.

Suddenly they both heard loud footsteps running across the landing. When they hurried up the stairs to investigate, they found the lights upstairs on and bedroom doors had been flung open, with the lights in those rooms also switched on. Yet there was no sign of anyone and there certainly was no evidence of anyone entering or leaving the building.

The lights in those rooms were switched off, doors that had been opened were then locked as a precaution against the possibility of an intruder being in the building and the proprietor was called. He arrived very quickly with his dog and a thorough search was made.

As they went upstairs they found that those doors that had been locked were now flung open and the lights that the deputy manager had switched off were back on. The dog became very excited and darted in and out of the rooms as though she was on a scent. But no one was ever found. The hotel was empty. Or was it?

Two years later on Christmas Eve, or the early hours of Christmas Day, and the festive season's celebrations were beginning to abate. The streets had fallen silent and Neath was beginning to sleep. The assistant and duty managers were bringing their work to an end and were sitting in the reception area.

The silence of the hotel was rudely broken by the sound of someone or something running across the upstairs landing. There was no one else in the building and following a full search, no one was found on the premises. But as in 1998, were they actually alone?

Edwardian Boy

On several occasions the night porters have reported seeing a boy dressed in Edwardian clothes roaming around the Castle Bar. There is no explanation for this sighting, the lad causes no harm, looks mortal but disappears from sight the second you look away. Look back to where he was standing and he is gone.

Lady in Black

One of the most persistent hauntings is that of a tall lady dressed entirely in black. She has been seen late at night walking down the main staircase and out through the main door. The doors seem to fly open without being touched and the woman disappears into the street.

Disturbances

It seems that the ghosts in the hotel don't like any alterations being carried out to the structure of the building. During a recent hotel refurbishment glasses were seen flying from shelves at the rear of the bar, which was the original site of the Nelson Bar.

The Cellars

The cellars under the restaurant area of the hotel were once used as the living quarters for the servants. These rooms haven't been used for many, many years and are now only accessible via trapdoor. When you descend into them you can see clear evidence of the beginning of what is believed to be a tunnel that connects to the River Neath.

The arch at the beginning of the tunnel was filled in with rubble years ago and most of the rooms in the cellar are filled in with rubble or have been bricked up. One of the main uses of the tunnel was to smuggle wines and rum and other goods from the river to the hotel.

Naturally now it is dank, dark and unwelcoming. Diners in the restaurant have on occasions mentioned that they thought they heard the sound of a dog howling. In the past there have been stories of people seeing a wolf like creature (probably a large dog) wandering around the cellar area when it was in use. Whatever, the diners' appetites do not diminish and they continue to patronise the hotel.

The Headless Cavalier

This is a very recent sighting. Pat Ellis, the lounge and restaurant manageress, told me that a gentleman in his mid-seventies was sitting quietly by one of the tables near the front windows in the lounge, drinking coffee and reading his newspaper. The area was reasonably quiet on that afternoon. Pat said that you wouldn't imagine that he was given to making extreme statements, but he said to her that he had seen a seemingly solid figure of a man sitting on an adjacent table dressed in seventeenth-century period clothing.

Pat told me that he had said he was reading the paper and out of the corner of his eye he saw the feet of this figure and immediately thought it strange. His eye line moved higher and when he got to this figure's neck, it appeared that he was headless. The gentleman then lowered his paper in surprise to get a better look and as he looked at it, the apparition disappeared.

Pat said that he wasn't fazed by the experience and still regularly comes into the lounge for his coffee and to peruse his newspaper.

James Rees, the proprietor of the Castle, said that this was the first report of this particular ghost.

The cellars of the Castle Hotel.

This room was once called the Nelson Room. It is now dedicated to the Welsh Rugby Union and is the site of many strange disturbances.

The Star Inn, Penydre

The landlord, Mr Peter Rees, willingly described to me the supernatural happenings that have been felt in the Star. This inn is one of the oldest licensed hostelries in Neath. First referenced in the late 1700s it is believed to have been built partially from stones taken from Neath Castle.

The subject of the haunting is said to be a lady, one Jane Thomas, who was born in the inn in 1865 and was the granddaughter of the landlord. Mr Rees said that he had not actually seen the ghost but he had felt a presence.

'I have felt a hand on my back,' he said, 'and sometimes you get the feeling that someone is close to you. When I felt the hand on my back I was sitting in the room and I turned around quickly but there was no one there. I was sitting with my back to the wall so no one could have been behind me and there was no draft or a chill in the air.'

Mr Rees' son said that he too had experienced an atmosphere and was convinced that there was something there.

The Star Inn, Penydre.

Mr Rees continued saying that several of his regulars had seen a shadowy figure moving about in the bar. 'A previous landlord has seen her,' he said. 'Other customers had seen it too, one claimed that when he had visited the toilet he saw a woman dressed in old fashioned clothes standing in the corner of the room. This person then said that the woman had walked through the wall.'

Some locals have said that the ghost may not be Jane Thomas, she didn't pass away on the premises, she died about 1897 and is buried in Swansea. Mr Rees added that some locals say the ghost is that of a woman who was murdered in a cottage next door to the inn.

Mr Rees is philosophical about the spirit. 'Many locals have talked about this story for years,' he said. 'Long before my time here. But whatever, if it is Jane Thomas trying to rekindle either a happy or a sad childhood and comes back or whether it is the ghost of a murdered lady who lived close by, I don't have a problem with it. I'm happy to share the place with her.'

The Victoria Inn

The Victoria, in Commercial Street, was the public house that preceded the Dark Arch and has since been renamed the Arch. In 1983 the building was being renovated and was owned by the late Mr Mike Richards.

Mr Richards had a contract with a Skewen joinery firm called the Wood Shop to make alterations and create a new bar in an upstairs room in the pub. The landlord was keen that this work should be carried out during the night to cause as little disruption as possible to the ongoing business.

Peter Williams was, and still is, employed as a carpenter by the Wood Shop and was briefed with carrying out the work. Peter had no problem with working at night. Then he had no opinion about ghosts or hauntings and as a twenty-year-old would usually laugh about such stories. But that was soon to change.

The Victoria dates back to the nineteenth century and was, not unusually, named after Queen Victoria. Its location places it very near the old animal market,

The site of the Victoria Inn, now called the Arch.

so it would have been frequented on market days by hundreds of farmers who gathered in the town to buy and sell their stock. It would have been used, too, by seafarers who would have been employed on ships that would have moored at one of the quays just below the Neath River bridge. A road is still there called Quay Road. The pub was also used by the Catholic Church before 1868 to hold services before they had a purpose-built building. The priests used one of the upstairs rooms to conduct Mass. The church moved after that date to what is now called the Moose Hall and stayed there until St Joseph's Church was opened in 1933.

Peter and a colleague soon got started on the work after the pub had closed and nothing happened on the first night to alarm them. They estimated the work would take a few nights.

On the second night, at just after 2.30 a.m., Peter was alone in the upstairs room. His mate had gone to the van to pick up some tools, when suddenly the temperature dramatically dropped to such a degree that he started to shiver. He couldn't explain this as the weather was warm. But he continued working and had his back to the bar that was under construction. There was a shelf holding a row of full bottles – the bottles started to rattle against each other, without falling off the shelf, creating quite a noise. Peter looked, unable to believe his eyes. The temperature was by now icy cold and the noise got louder and louder.

He said he just stared at the bottles. 'I was scared', he said. 'But I know what I saw. Then strangely from behind me or to my side, I can't even now say from where, there was a sort of muffled scream, as though you screamed into a handkerchief or a cloth. Muffled. I moved to the door, turned and ran down the stairs. I was shaking, told my mate to get in van. I slammed the pub door and we left, quickly. I suppose to use the cliché, I was white. Later that morning I told my boss about the experience and that I was not going back there during the night.'

Peter's boss, then as now, was Brian Richards (no relation to Mike Richards, the landlord) and he got in touch with Mike and explained what had happened. The landlord was understanding, saying that previous contractors who had worked in the room had related a similar story. Mike went on to say that a seaman, lodging in the pub sometime during the late 1800s, had been robbed and murdered in that room.

I haven't yet checked the validity of this crime but I will and maybe then we will throw more light on this unhappy ghost.

Peter and his mate continued the renovations during the daytime and despite there being no further disruption to their work, he said he was glad when the job was finished. And, defensively, he adds, 'I know what I saw.'

Five

LLANTWIT CEMETERY

The Playmate

Like millions of other people throughout the country, Josie Thomas always acknowledged the anniversaries in her late father's life by placing flowers on his grave in Llantwit Cemetery.

The Victorian–Edwardian municipal cemetery stands on elevated ground overlooking the town, and typical for that period, the graves vary in elegance and pomp from large, monolithic edifices with the names in fading gold lettering, to the more humble kerb surrounds with the names merely etched into the stone.

The grave of Jack Thomas, died 21 May 1958, was more like the latter, with earth in its centre but there was a modest headstone.

Josie, her husband David and their two year old daughter Meryl were busily arranging the flowers to mark the day her dad had died. He had been gone twenty years to the day.

David had left Josie to go and fill the pot with water from a communal tap, while Meryl had wandered some way down the path. Josie was busy cutting the stems of the flowers to the correct size and was chatting away, hoping that her father might just be listening.

David arrived back and put the pot into its marble holder in the centre of the grave and he helped Josie by handing her the flowers. It was a lovely day with

Llantwit Cemetery.

the warm sun filtering through the high trees on the cemetery's periphery. It was nearly 5.30 p.m.

There was no one else in sight; Meryl was prancing about, playing a little further down the path. They looked at her and smiled.

They concentrated again on tidying the grave. Josie wiped the stone with a damp cloth and David pulled up a few weeds from the side. After about fifteen minutes they put the scissors and cloth back into the bag and stood up, preparing themselves to leave.

'Meryl,' David shouted. 'Come on.'

The child had wandered a little further away but not far enough to cause them concern. She was though two or three graves in from the path and David worried she might fall. 'Come on,' he repeated.

The child was singing and dancing around and trying to string together the few words she was getting used to.

'You'll have to go and get her,' said Josie.

'No, we'll walk back through the bottom gate, we'll pick her up as we pass,' said David.

Carefully they stepped along the side of those graves adjacent to her father's until they were safely on the path. 'Meryl, we are going,' Josie called.

This time the child looked towards them. Her face was beaming. She looked back to where she had been playing and said quiet clearly, 'Bye, I'll come again to play.'

David felt a shiver run through him. He understood just how literal children of Meryl's age were. Josie and David were now close to Meryl when the child turned and again said, 'I'm going with my mammy and daddy now.'

The parents looked at each other. The child ran to them and took her father's hand, 'Who were you waving to?' David asked.

'My friend,' she said.

'Let's get out of here, David,' said Josie.

'He said his name is Ben,' said Meryl smiling.

David picked up the child, took Josie's hand and they hurried from the cemetery.

Some weeks later David attended a funeral in the new section of Llantwit Cemetery and following the service, as other mourners made their way home, he walked down along the path not far from his father-in-law's grave, to the point where Meryl had been playing. There he saw a headstone, reading 'In Memory of our darling son Ben – Born 21 May 1976 – Died 21 May 1978.' The child had died on his second birthday, though there were no flowers on the grass-covered grave, only a wooden cross. He shared dates with Josie's father. He was also Meryl's friend.

Family Members?

Another incident told to me recently was concerning a family whose forebears originated from Neath but had moved to Cornwall. Three of them were holidaying in South Wales and took the opportunity to visit the town to try and track down and find the graves of their ancestors. They found themselves in Llantwit Cemetery on a fine Saturday afternoon in May 2005.

Armed with pens, notebooks, a camera and a list of deceased names they were, as far as they knew, alone in the graveyard and independently searched from grave to grave reading the inscriptions.

After about two hours one of them found a match and excitedly called to the others who hurried towards him. Repeatedly they checked the details against those in their notes and were convinced they had discovered some of their family. They carefully placed tracing paper against the words and crayoned the image, which transferred the inscriptions of the five members who had lain resting there for the past 100 years.

Each taking a drink from their flasks, they sat on the edge of the grave delighted at the discovery. One of the paths that divided the graves into sections was only some 25ft from them when quite suddenly three people appeared to them. Initially they didn't react but merely smiled and waved a greeting. The three people waved and smiled with a great deal of enthusiasm. One wore a black top hat. With the suddenness that they appeared, they vanished. One of the Cornish visitors who, together with his companions, asked me to withhold their names, said:

> They didn't just walk away slowly – people tend to walk slowly in cemeteries, don't they? – they vanished. Only then did we realise that this was strange. But they acknowledged us like we belonged. You know, like you have bumped into a long time friend or someone from your family. We think they were three ghosts, and they belonged to us.
>
> The strange thing is that even after we realised we'd seen something spooky we were not frightened. One had a top hat on and they all were dressed in old clothes – I mean old from a different time.

One if the intrepid searchers said that it's a pity they hadn't take a photo.

A pity indeed, but they returned to Cornwall convinced that members of their past family are active in a haunted Neath.

Six

POLTERGEISTS

Mayhem in a Tonna House

Poltergeists, or mischievous ghosts, are generally thought to be the spirits of children. They have a tendency to throw inanimate objects about and generally cause mayhem, often resulting in terrifying people.

Such was the haunting in a council house in Tonna in 2002. The three-bedroom house was built in the 1950s and was occupied by a woman in her late thirties and her ten year old son at the time of the malevolent behaviour. There had recently been a bitter marital break up and the husband had left the home.

Three weeks after the domestic problems the son was awoken one evening when a cuddly teddy bear seemed to push itself down into the bedclothes alongside him. The room was in darkness and the mother was in her own room asleep.

Now awake, the child pulled the toy from the bedclothes and put it on the end of the bed. He was sitting up – only streetlights cast any break in the darkness, throwing shadows across the bedroom – when the teddy, apparently thrown, hit him in the face. He cried out for his mother and ran to her room.

She took him into her bed thinking it was another bad dream. Like many children he'd had mysterious, nocturnal 'friends'. She cuddled him and soon they fell asleep.

The house in Tonna is located along the righr-hand turning.

In the morning he did remember the incident, but his mother convinced him it was a 'bad dream' and soon he was taken to school. When the mother returned she busied herself around the house; the boy's bedroom was the last room she started to put straight. The teddy bear was on the floor in a corner but some ornaments that had always been on the dressing room table were scattered around the floor. Although annoyed, she put this down to her son playing with them.

She made the bed and put the items back where they belonged and as she left the room she thought she saw a shadow passing along a wall. Startled, she turned quickly but saw nothing. She told herself not to be stupid and closed the door.

That night the boy went to bed as usual and slept through without any disturbance. But about midnight the woman awoke; she could hear a light sound coming from the kitchen. Her throat became dry as she quickly became fully awake. She concentrated on the sound. A clink, clink, clink at regular intervals.

Annoyed and possessive about her home, she got out of bed and quietly opened the boy's bedroom. Everything seemed fine, the lad was fast asleep. She followed the sound down the stairs, went through the living room, noticing that she had left the television on although she thought she had turned it off at the mains, which was what she usually did, and entered the kitchen. The clinking sound was clearly audible now. Her hand on the light switch, she illuminated the room.

With utter relief the sound was emanating from the washing machine and the clinking sound was nothing more than a button or a zip touching the interior of the machine. She had activated the machine before going to bed.

She made tea and sat awhile before returning to bed, turning the television off as she went through the living room.

The following morning the boy awoke and told his mother the teddy bear was in bed with him again last night.

'That's nice,' she said, 'keeps you company, doesn't it?'

'Yes,' he said, 'but I didn't put him there. He was on the floor when I went to sleep.'

This did concern the mother who remembered her nocturnal visit to the kitchen, but she didn't elaborate on what her son had said.

For the next week or so unusual behaviour centred on the teddy but nothing else happened. The television had remained off, and she was consciously aware when she pulled out the plugs. But her son complained about the bear and on a Sunday night after tucking him up in bed for the night, about nine o'clock, she said, 'Shall I take teddy to my room?'

He smiled and agreed.

Before long, as she sat watching television, there was a loud bang coming from her son's bedroom followed by him screaming. She switched all the lights on and ran up the stairs, two steps at a time shouting that she was there. When she went to open the child's bedroom door it refused to move. Her son was screaming and there was another bang. She was panic stricken.

'Can you open the door?' she shouted.

He didn't answer but she swears she heard a laugh, which was her son's voice. She banged her shoulder against the door but it remained fast. She ran back down the stairs and out of the front door screaming. She crossed the lawn and glanced up at her son's bedroom window, where the lights were flashing on and off with great rapidity. This room had only a switch on the wall that the son could only just reach. The was no pull-cord. He couldn't be responsible for the light being tuned on and off with such speed.

She banged the next door neighbour's door and continued screaming. The neighbour was a man of substantial build and wasn't easily frightened of anything. He told her to be quiet and asked her what was the matter. She couldn't speak coherently but uttered, 'Come and help.'

As they crossed the lawn back to her neat semi-detached house, the lights were still flashing on and off and they could hear the child crying loudly, pitifully.

The neighbour asked again as he followed her, 'What's going on?'

Up the stairs she went and again as she tried to open the bedroom door it wouldn't move. The neighbour watched incredulously and knew that it should open with ease.

'Out of the way,' he said and it took three powerful attempts of his shoulder crashing against it before it opened. 'There must be something jammed against it,' he said. 'What the heck has been going on?'

As they entered the room the lights has stopped flashing and it was in darkness. There was nothing obstructing the door. There was, of course, no lock. The lad could be heard sobbing. His mother went to put the light on and pulled her fingers away quickly. The switch was very hot. Too hot to touch. The neighbour did though press the switch down and the room lit up.

What they saw was breathtaking. The lad was sitting in a corner of the room, his eyes were open wide, staring, he wasn't crying now; the dressing table was upside down jammed between the wall and the bed, the small wardrobe was in its usual position but tuned around so that the door was against the wall, and pictures were laying around with the glass smashed.

The mother picked up the child and held him close. The neighbour was astonished, and asked what had been going on? He had asked this question a few times.

She carried the child down the stairs and sat in the living room cuddling him. She then, albeit disjointedly, tried to relate what had been going on.

'You can't stay here tonight,' he said. 'Have you somewhere to go, your parents, sister, brother?'

She shook her head, crying.

'Right then, come into our house. We'll try and sort things tomorrow but we should get this boy to a doctor, he's badly shocked,' he said.

The neighbour's wife had been roused by all the noise and her husband carried the boy into the house. 'Call a doctor,' he said.

By the time the doctor arrived the child had settled a little. In different surroundings and with his mother and the neighbours, he felt less threatened.

The doctor advised the boy be given mild painkilling tablets that would induce sleep. These did work and soon the child was asleep on the settee. The mother stayed with him sitting in an armchair. She didn't sleep at all.

The following morning they entered her house and everything in the boy's bedroom was in the same chaos. The neighbour managed to get the place reasonably straight and the theory about a noisy ghost did seem like the only explanation. How could the door have failed to open? He had taken several attempts to shoulder it; the light switch was very hot, the wardrobe turned the wrong way, the dressing table seemingly thrown to get jammed between the bed and the wall, pictures and glass everywhere. It took him most of the morning to tidy up.

The mother was linking all this activity to the teddy bear, which she had taken into her room. She checked her room looking for it but it was nowhere to be found.

The neighbour realising that help of a more spiritual nature was needed, and needed quickly, phoned a friend who was familiar with certain members of the clergy. The priest called a few hours later and listened to the happenings before performing the rite of exorcism.

A friend of the mother agreed to come and stay with her following the religious rite and all was calm afterwards in the house.

But alarmingly, a few weeks later the teddy bear, which hadn't been seen since the mother took it to her room before the disturbance, appeared on the roof of the house. It was lying against the slates and the guttering. Just lying there.

This house had no unseemly past. Since it was built nothing of a sinister nature had happened there, and certainly nothing that would cause the presence of anything supernatural to frequent the house.

The mother arranged new accommodation immediately for both her son and herself and won't even enter the village, let alone the street, which had once housed her home.

Peter the Poltergeist

A similar story was told to me in 1989 by a young woman who had returned to Neath to live. Her experience was whilst she had been working in Berkshire and lived in a place called Chepstow Cottage. The cottage was on a large estate and all the small dwellings were named after racecourses. She was so familiar with the ghost that her and her friends who shared the cottage called him Peter the Poltergeist, and would chastise him for his wrongdoings when he was active. Strangely enough, he wasn't threatening or destructive. But those who lived in the place were convinced of his presence.

One Saturday evening she had been alone in the cottage, as the other two girls who shared the place had gone home for the weekend. The television was playing up, it would change channels without the remote control being used and would sometimes just leave a fuzzy noise as though there was interference.

She did what everyone did and told Peter to behave himself. The television retuned to normal. Then she decided to take a bath and whist soaking in the water a blue, plastic bowl went careering across the room and fell to the floor. This alarmed her and as she climbed out of the bath it again was 'thrown' from one side of the room to the other.

Hurriedly she put a towel around herself and let the water out of the bath. The television was still on but again the channels changed. She phoned her father.

He was 200 miles away; the couple who lived next door were away. The father suggested she tell Peter to behave again and that she should go to bed.

'I know it's an odd story but with Peter there was no malevolent feeling. Those of us who lived in the cottage believed that a child must have died there at some time. The cottages were dating back to the 1700s. People who had lived there before us also told us about things being moved and the television going on and off. My father had a theory that the television disturbance could be related to the fact that the estate was immediately below the flight path from Heathrow to the United States of America and the planes wouldn't have been airborne very long and would be climbing rapidly so perhaps something technical was interfering with the set. But the blue bowl was nothing to do with aeroplanes or technology going wonky. I was on my own, save for the cat, and it stopped when I told Peter the Poltergeist to behave himself.'

Seven

OUTSIDE THE TOWN

The Boatman

It was one of those delightful, warm, endless June days in 1968 when John Morgan, his wife Susan and their one-year-old son James (not their real names) decided to spend a quiet afternoon on Morfa Beach in Margam.

Morfa Beach was, as was usual, deserted. The area, within sight of the Port Talbot Steel Works, was a haven for courting couples. This day, though, only the gulls dallied in tandem. A light breeze cooled the family as they sat on a blanket eating a picnic, watching the sea, enjoying the peace and delighting in the baby.

The family had no strong beliefs in anything. They lived quietly; John, a bus driver, supported his family, only occasionally visiting the pub. They kept themselves very much within the home.

After the picnic had been cleared away, drawing patterns in the sand and playing with James, John decided to have a swim. He hadn't eaten anything from the picnic and was a strong swimmer.

He stripped to his trunks and told Susan he wouldn't be long and that he wouldn't swim out too far. She was used to this because whenever they visited the beach he took full advantage of the water.

The sea wasn't cold, but was cool enough to be really refreshing. He hadn't been to Morfa for years. He walked in up to his chest and rolled into the water, submerging himself and tasting the salt, he felt rejuvenated. Slowly he resurfaced and with powerful, measured strokes he pulled his fourteen stone frame forward.

After about five or six minutes he rolled on to his back and floated; watching the wheeling gulls, feeling the gentle breeze brush across his face. The smell of salt was delightful. Above the gentle waves he could just make out Susan on the beach. He swam further out and allowed the swell of the water to aid his progress. He turned when he estimated he was about half a mile from the shore and trod water. He was feeling strong and confident. The isolation was a welcome relief from the daily chore of driving on a fare stage bus route.

He glanced along the rugged line of the coast; it bobbed in and out of his sight with the rise and fall of the waves. A little way to his right were the Sker Rocks, the scene of the *Santampa* disaster in 1947, when the entire crew of the Mumbles lifeboat were lost. Nearby, too, was the place where the *Amazon* had been blown aground with the loss of nineteen souls. A little further along the coast was the site of Sker House and the romantic story of the Maid of Sker. Mulling over these thoughts, John decided to swim back to the beach. He allowed the swell to carry him shoreward when he felt the muscle in his right leg stiffen. He realised he had cramp. He stroked the water gently and instinctively floated. He realised the tide was taking him further out. He felt the pangs of fear as he realised his problem. His swimming teacher's words echoed in his mind. 'Relax. Relax.'

Nevertheless his breath became sharper. Then his left leg cramped, too, and from a floating position his weight was pulled down to a vertical one. He knew he was in serious trouble.

His thoughts flashed to Susan and James. He began to thrash about. He tried to be calm and move both his arms in unison in the water to keep his head above the sea. His breathing was much more laboured and the pain in his legs was excruciating. The water that had always been his friend had turned nasty as it carried him further away from the shore, indeed, he could hardly see the beach. Isolation, from earlier being his friend, was now his enemy.

Still the gulls wheeled and called, clouds scudded across blue sky. Unheralded thoughts entered his mind, he was very fatigued and in intense pain. In absolute desperation he shouted, 'Help me, someone. Help me!'

The shore was out of his sight when to his left-hand side a boat appeared, being rowed by a man dressed in a white shirt. John thrashed about trying vainly to grab at it.

The boat manoeuvred closer to him. 'Don't try and get in,' the boatman said. 'hold the stern and I will tow you to the shore.'

As the stern was within his grasp he lurched at it, his head only just above the water. With both his hands on the boat he was able to raise his body just below the water as the boat rowed slowly forward.

John gripped so much his knuckles were like a white line, but he was conscious of a stinging pain in his left hand and could see a small line of blood. He had hit a splinter but that naturally did not worry him. Now he was being taken to safety. He was oblivious to the identity of the boatman and as the sand brushed his feet he let the boat go and scrambled on to the beach exhausted. He crawled towards Susan, who began to chastise him for being so long. 'I was getting worried,' she said.

'I had cramp,' he said between gulps of breath. 'I had cramp. I thought... Then a rowing boat came past and towed me in...'

'Rowing boat?' said Susan. 'What rowing boat? There is no boat; you have just crawled out of the water.'

John was incredulous and looked at the sea. There was nothing to be seen. But the boat should still have been in sight. And Susan must have seen it. 'I was towed in,' he said fighting back tears as shock started to set in. 'The man said to hold on to the stern. I can remember...'

'What have you done to your hand?' asked Susan taking hold of it. A steady stream of blood trickled along the lines of his palm. She absorbed the blood with a handkerchief. Then he remembered the sharp pain he felt when he caught hold of the boat.

'I got a splinter or something when I grabbed the boat,' he said. She looked at him quizzically.

Susan poured him tea from the flask and put a plaster on his hand. The bleeding had stopped. Then a cool breeze sprang up making them both shiver. James began to cry.

'Come on,'said Susan, 'we had better go.'

John quickly dressed and they made their way back to their parked car. They both turned and gazed at the sea. It was a little choppier than when they arrived. But no vessel could be seen anywhere.

John knew he had been saved, but by whom?

Margam Castle.

Margam Castle

Following an article I had written in the *Neath Guardian* some years ago on ghost hunting and hauntings in general, Alan Wilson, the acclaimed author who lives in Bryncoch, wrote to me describing an experience he had witnessed in Margam Castle in 1943. During the Second World War the mansion was requisitioned by the government for the billeting of services' personnel.

In Mr Wilson's words:

I had a haunting experience in Margam Castle back in February 1943. The building still had some furniture and wallpaper then. We were young soldier lads aged about nineteen and twenty years and were billeted in the castle. We slept on the bare boards wrapped in our blankets. My mates and I were in a large room at the top of the main stairs in the old part of the place.

About midnight a chap rushed into our room in terror saying he had seen a ghost. We all laughed at him, but then a strong radiance grew (although we had just one candle) and a damp chill permeated the room, giving a most menacing feeling and a terrible sense of foreboding. Some of the chaps hid their heads underneath their blankets.

Eventually the light cleared and many of the lads refused to stay another night in the room and decamped to the Orangery below the mansion, which was located near the Abbey. I remained in the room with a few others and the following night, precisely at 12 o'clock the same thing happened again, the radiance of light grew and was accompanied by the dread and foreboding. All of us felt scared for our souls. After that we all moved into the Orangery and experienced no further trouble whatsoever.

In 1977 the mansion was gutted by fire and Mr Wilson wonders whether this event exorcised the building of its ghostly presence?

The Gamekeeper

Regarding Margam Castle, one story that does persist is that of the ghost of a gamekeeper called Robert Scott who it is said was murdered in the grounds in the late 1890s.

Whilst taking a group of local history students around both the abbey and the castle some years ago I met a gentleman, then in his late eighties. He was very

The stairwell at Margam Castle where a ghostly maid has been seen descending.

View of the stairwell, Margam Castle.

passionate about the area and clearly very keen on the subject of ghosts in general and particularly those that frequented the site, which is now owned by Neath Port Talbot County Borough Council and is used for public recreation.

He elaborated on Robert Scott and said that he had indeed seen him on numerous occasions in the grounds and near the back entrance of the castle. He's dressed in typical Victorian gamekeepers' clothes he said, down to the deerstalker. He always has a stout staff with him and sometimes a black and white spaniel. He always looks preoccupied but never threatening. 'You wouldn't realise he was a ghost if it were not for his old fashioned clothes and that once both he and his dog disappeared in front of me. Then I knew and to be honest with you, I was quite delighted.'

He mentioned other hauntings, too, such as the strange echo-like singing of voices, probably children in a downstairs room of the castle. 'The first time I heard this,' he said, 'I walked normally to the room because I thought that it was a school or something giving children a tour. But when I pushed open the door it was completely empty and the singing stopped abruptly.'

He went on telling me about a maid that he had seen coming down the stairs carrying a tray of dishes. 'She, too, had that solid appearance and I did acknowledge her once but there was no reaction and she disappeared before she got to the bottom of the stairs. I've seen her a few times.'

The site of the Abbey dates back to the twelfth century when the monks were granted a charter to set up a monastery. They became members of the Cistercian Order and the monks' activities only ceased there following the Reformation in 1536.

The castle, a Gothic pile, was built in 1827 by the Talbots. Margam Park, together with the castle, was purchased by Sir David Evans Bevan in 1942. The estate was then purchased in 1973 by the now defunct Glamorgan County Council, then transferred on local government reorganisation to the equally defunct West Glamorgan County Council. It is now the responsibility of Neath Port Talbot County Borough Council.

On the site there is also an Iron Age camp, which would have been occupied by members of the Silures, the tribe who put up the initial resistance to the conquering Claudian Roman Army from AD 43. The Roman road runs quite close to the site.

Also, romantically located above the abbey and castle, is Capel Mair, a church built by the monks to facilitate worship for the farming lay population. Once a year there is a Catholic service held there to mark the feast of John Lloyd, who was executed in Cardiff after being found guilty of holding Mass in Sker House.

So I understand the enthusiasm of our gentleman friend; Margam Abbey and castle has experienced many layers of life, so the crossing over from one time to another by those who have failed to find a lasting peace can excite many who are interested in events of a spooky nature.

The Airman

Following various government schemes the Neath Canal between Resolven and Aberpergwm has been cleaned, the stone work on the bridges and the locks repainted, in places rebuilt and the tow path relaid, making the area a pleasant and easy walk.

Late in August 1998 John and Barbara Williams were getting to know the area having moved into the valley from Llannon in Carmarthenshire. They had brought with them their five month old puppy, Bron, who walked quietly on the lead.

The Neath Canal near Resolven where the ghostly figure of an airman has been seen.

They passed Ty Banc, one of the few dwellings left from the days when the canal was a busy highway with barges hauling cargo from Pontwalby to Neath and to Briton Ferry. Now the building was used as a coffee shop by a children's charity. The sun was setting, throwing shards of light through the trees and the air was warm; it was a wonderful day for walking. The old A465 road, now called the B4242 runs parallel to the canal and traffic is clearly seen driving past. Drivers can also see people walking on the tow path.

As they passed the lock opposite Rheola they both saw a figure coming towards them. This was not unusual as anyone who has walked the canal will tell you. It is a well used area for gentle recreation.

He was dressed in combat clothes, the type you can buy in Army surplus stores. On his head he wore a leather helmet, little used today, above his forehead were a pair of goggles, he wore leather gloves, and on his feet were substantial leather boots. He was walking towards them studying a map. Apart from what appeared to be eccentric clothes for such an evening, he looked normal. Though as John told me, on reflection his clothes were anything but normal. That evening everything was peaceful, warm and comfortable. You can be more tolerant of other people's eccentricity when you experience such conditions.

About three yards from us he stopped and looked at us. The puppy just stared at him, making no noise, which was unusual because whenever we met a stranger it was very yappy. He looked down at his map and looked at us again.

'Is this the Vale of Neath?' he asked in a northern English accent.

'Yes,' I said.

He nodded and traced his finger along the map. 'I've ditched,' he said.

'Ditched? How do you mean?' I asked.

'My glider,' he replied. 'I've come down a few fields away, back there,' he said looking around.

'Are you hurt?' I asked him.

He shook his head. 'No. but I must find a phone. How far is the nearest village?'

'Half a mile,' I said. 'Resolven.'

I was in the habit of always carrying a small flask of tea. even if only going on a short walk. I offered him a swig from the flask. He thanked me and did drink it. Barbara throughout this conversation said nothing but added to the story by saying that his eyes were strange. They seemed to have a defect; he also pursed his lips constantly. But this does happen, but you never comment on it. He thanked us for the tea and continued down the tow path. Then it occurred to me that I had in my pocket a mobile phone. I hadn't possessed it very long and was still not used to using it.

'I got this now,' I said to Barbara feeling in my pocket and produced the mobile. 'He can phone on it.'

We both turned to call him but there was no sign of him. The tow path has no bends at this point and he couldn't have walked more than twenty yards. But there was nothing or no one to be seen. The puppy still stared, with its head inclined the way the airman had gone. We walked on only for about five minutes before turning back. About half a mile along the path another couple were walking towards us. I acknowledged them and asked if they had seen a man dressed in combat clothes with a leather helmet on his head. They looked surprised and said that no one had passed them.

A day or so later one of John's friends said that he had seen them standing just above the Rheola Lock as he drove down the valley. When asked if he'd seen anyone with them, he had said he hadn't.

At the top end of the valley there is a gliding club in the village of Rhigos. John checked if anyone had been flying from there on that evening. He was told that on the days before he saw the airman and after the club had been closed. There had been no aircraft movement at all.

The couple often muse about the incident wondering just what they had seen. 'When he took the cup from me we didn't touch,' said John. 'He just took it from me, took a sip and gave it back.'

Did they on that quiet unassuming evening meet a glider pilot caught in time? Maybe from the Second World War? Gliders were used. And the area south of the Brecon Beacons was used for training. Did he come off course and crash? Does this lost pilot haunt the Neath Canal?

The Collecting Mists

This section contains actual experiences that both local people and visitors to the area have had whilst travelling on the road between Aberdulais and Aberpergwm. This was notoriously dangerous and called the A465. Since the opening of the new bypass in 1998, the road has had its status downgraded and was reclassified as the B4242. Along its length there are several hamlets, still self-contained and not affected by the disease inflicted upon us by the city fathers of ribbon development that so often erodes communities. Sections of the road have altered and haven't always been where they are today: the outline of track at the side of the road between Ynysarwed, Abergarwed, behind the Farmers' Arms (Ynysybibbin in Alexandra Cordell's 'Song of the Earth') and to a point running in front of the nineteenth century Rheola House was once the main thoroughfare.

Before the bypass it was exceptionally busy, as it was the main route linking the Heads of the Valleys to Neath and Swansea and even busier before the opening of the M4, which did lighten the traffic by carrying many of the heavy vehicles that were bound for West Wales. But even after the M4 was opened, the Neath Valley road was always subject to constant heavy traffic.

Accidents and death were this road's bedfellows. Many argued that it was one of the most dangerous highways in Wales. Several people have had unusual and seemingly inexplicable experiences whilst driving and walking along it.

The Swirling Mist

Peter Carey worked in Aberdare and lived in Birchgrove, thus used the road on almost a daily basis. He told me that he had driven along the road for nearly twenty years, both during the daytime and at night. Never given to fanciful thoughts

The B4242 where collecting, swirling mists have terrified motorists.

regarding spirits, he was always focused on the driving and had never been involved in any sort of accident.

One January morning in 1974 he was on his way to work. He passed the Rock and Fountain public house about six o'clock. He was in good time and was driving about 40mph. There were no other vehicles about. As he negotiated the bends before entering the hamlet of Ynysarwed he drove suddenly into a bank of heavy swirling mist. He wasn't panicked by this, he had encountered it before. The road is level with the River Neath, you are on a flood plain, and in the right temperature the conditions often causes heavy mists to gather.

Peter dipped his headlights to offset the glare, which bounced back at him and he decelerated. He inclined himself forward in the driving seat trying peer through the gloom. Normally the mist lasted for a few yards, fifty at most, before clearing. This time, though, it seemed to get thicker and took on a whitish colour; there seemed no end to it. He had virtually stopped the car, the mist had enveloped him, and it was freezing cold, despite the car's heater belting out hot air. Then the engine failed. He jabbed the accelerator trying to feel that reassuring pressure under his foot that provided momentum to the car. It ground to a halt as the mist began to swirl around alarmingly.

He remembers a drowsiness coming over him; he fought the feeling of tiredness and tried to start the car but remembers the frustration as the key turned lifelessly in the ignition. He believes that he then fell asleep.

When he woke up, Peter remembered the mist but it had completely cleared. It was daylight. Yet his watch still told him the time was five past six. And the car was moving as though it had not stopped, there was other traffic behind him, in front of him and coming towards him. He felt a tingling feeling in his arms and legs but apart from that he felt all right. The time on his watch intrigued him. On his right there was a Shell petrol station. He pulled in.

The old gentleman came out of his cabin to serve him. Peter wound the window down and asked him the time. 'Coming up to ten o'clock,' he said. He had lost four hours. His watch had stopped, so still read five past six.

'I was both upset and feeling very shaky,' he told me some twenty-five years after the experience. 'What did happen?' No one can explain that. There are several instances of this time lapsing recorded but none can be satisfactorily explained.

Peter said that when he arrived at work his boss was understandably annoyed about his lateness. 'And to cap it all,' said Peter, 'he docked me four hours pay. I was supposed to start work at seven and arrived at eleven.'

He said that he had never again used that section of road during darkness. 'I would drive through Tonna and Melin Court and come out at Resolven. It was a relief to me when I found work in Swansea.' And the watch? 'I kept that,' he said, 'I never altered it.' He showed it to me. It was still reading five past six.

So be careful when you encounter mist on the old road through the valley, it might be some time before you come out the other side.

The Girl in the Red PVC Coat

This is one of the most unusual stories related to me and also one of the saddest. In the October of 2007 I was walking around Gorffwysfa Cemetery in Blaengwrach. This graveyard is one of the highest and most scenic in the Vale of Neath. It was a warm autumn evening and sitting on one of the benches was a man of about fifty years of age holding a bunch of flowers.

As I walked past I acknowledged him, and as I did so he asked if I had a light. I had a lighter and offered it to him. He put the flowers down and fumbled in his pocket for his packet of cigarettes.

'Thanks,' he said.

'Who are the flowers for?' I asked.

' My great aunt, I visit once a year and then go on to Melin Court Chapel to put another bunch on my brother's grave.'

The B4242 near Rheola where the girl in the red PVC coat was seen.

'Are you living in the valley?'

'No,' he said, 'after my brother died the family moved away. I live in Worcester. Have done for many years.'

I sat next to him and he told me a sad story:

It was in 1961, my brother Dai was driving his newly acquired Hillman Minx on the road between Pentreclwydau and Resolven. It was nearly midnight and pouring with rain. The car's headlights picked up a girl walking towards Resolven, her head into her umbrella trying to gain as much protection as possible from the weather.

A few yards past her Dai pulled up and opened the passenger door. 'Get in,' he said. The girl looked into the car and thanked him and jumped in, her PVC coat soaking the seat and her umbrella soaking the floor. She said she was sorry about this.

She had dark brown hair and was very attractive. Dai said later that he hadn't recognised her. She told him she was living in Melin Court and Dai said, 'Just tell me the way, I'll drop you at your home.'

She proceeded to give him accurate directions and after they left Resolven they were soon pulling up outside her home, which was one of the few side streets in her village.

'This is it,' she said as she opened the door, 'thanks very much.'

'I'll watch you go into your house,' said Dai.

'Thanks, all right,' she said.

'Go on,' said Dai as he leaned on over with his hand on the passenger seat as he peered through the passenger door window. It's bloody soaking, he thought.

The girl opened the metal gate and it gently clanged behind her. She turned and waved briefly and smiled brilliantly as she turned towards the front door. And then, as Dai was watching her she disappeared. Like a light just went out, Dai had said.

He remained in the car for several minutes quite stunned before beginning to question what he had seen. Must have been mistaken, he had said. Then he decided to knock the door and ask if she was all right.

The house was in darkness, something that hadn't registered before with him. He gently tapped the metal knocker at first and when this didn't elicit a response he banged it harder. This did have the favoured result and a light came on and the door was opened.

It was the same girl. 'Yes,' she snapped. It was well past midnight and Dai was soaking by this time.

'Just wanted to make sure that you are all right,' he said, 'I didn't see you go into the house.'

Dai could see the red PVC coat hanging on a clothes peg inside the door. He did notice that is seemed perfectly dry.

'What do you mean?' she asked with an undisguised hint of annoyance in her voice.

'I gave you a lift home,' said Dai feeling decidedly uneasy.

'I haven't been out today at all,' she said. 'Now, please go, I don't know what you are playing at. My father's upstairs.'

Dai backed away, turned and hurried to the car. As he drove off he glanced at the house which was again in total darkness.

Dai's brother said that he told the story to several of his mates all of whom said he must have been drunk. And there it would have remained but for the fact that two weeks later a girl was killed on that section of road. When Dai saw a picture of the same girl he was never the same again.

He started to have nightmares and became obsessed with the car ride and the girl sitting in the passenger seat. He started to go out late at night and walk the hills and on more than one occasion he had been found wandering around one of the several cemeteries in the area and had to be brought home. He became withdrawn; his family were concerned about him. His mental health began to deteriorate and the local doctor suggested that he seek the help from a psychiatrist. This didn't help much and within six months Dai took his own life. He hanged himself in the woodland between Clyne and Tonna.

What Dai experienced on that fateful night when he picked up the girl remains a mystery. Had he hallucinated? He had indeed been drinking, but he was convinced that he had met the girl a few weeks before she had died and the picture appeared in a newspaper.

The White Lady

This ghost is called the White Lady, but those that have seen this apparition relate that what they see is a wisp of mist, in the shape of a lady, who walks always towards the canal on the path alongside Cadoxton Churchyard. I asked the late Miss Gertie Bowen about this story; Miss Bowen was one of the most respected ladies in the village and lived then in No. 4 Woodland Terrace. She told me she had heard the story, but in all her years had never seen the ghost. There is no real theory about who she is or indeed what it is.

The lady is always seen from a distance and some people in the area believe it could be the haunting of Margaret Williams, the subject of the Murder Stone.

Margaret was murdered in 1822, a maid from Carmarthenshire living in service at Gellia Farm on the lower slopes of Mynydd March Hywel. Included in her duties were driving the cattle to the marsh in the morning and then driving them back to the farm in the evening.

The lane near Cadoxton Church where the ghost of the White Lady has been witnessed.

One day she didn't return and her murdered body was found 'in a ditch below the churchyard'. She was found to be pregnant and the suspect was the son of the farmer for whom she worked. With little evidence against him he left soon after and emigrated to Canada or North America.

And so the story would have lain, just another working class girl very much down on her luck becoming the victim of a barbaric act. The villagers of Cadoxton felt strongly that the murderer had escaped and commissioned the local antiquarian, Elijah Waring to write a vengeful epitaph on her gravestone:

1823
TO RECORD

MURDER

THIS STONE WAS ERECTED
OVER THE BODY
OF
MARGARET WILLIAMS
AGED 26
A NATIVE OF CARMARTHENSHIRE
LIVING IN SERVICE IN THIS PARISH
WHO WAS FOUND DEAD
WITH MARKS OF VIOLENCE ON HER PERSON
IN A DITCH ON THE MARSH
BELOW THIS CHURCHYARD
ON THE MORNING
OF SUNDAY THE FOURTEENTH OF JULY
1822

ALTHOUGH
THE SAVAGE MURDERER
ESCAPED A SEASON THE DETECTION OF MAN
YET
THE CRY OF BLOOD
WILL ASSUREDLY PURSUE HIM
TO CERTAIN AND TERRIBLE RIGHTEOUS
JUDGEMENT

The Murder Stone, Cadoxton Church.

The stone has almost become a cliché in local history circles in Neath. It appears everywhere, in books, newspapers and magazines illustrating tales of murder and retribution. It isn't unique, there is one very similar in Nebo Chapel in Felindre, Swansea and there is one, I believe, in the Rhondda. The example in Felindre carries an almost identical epitaph and is dated from the same time as the one in Cadoxton. It is possible that Elijah Waring was the engraver responsible them both.

Could the white misty lady be Margaret Williams' ghost driving the cattle to their daily grazing ground? Has she been doing this for the past 180 years? Does she, indeed, know she is dead?

As a footnote to the Murder Stone story, about eight years ago I received a phone call asking if I would help some people from Canada who were tracing their roots in the Neath area. I willingly agreed.

I arranged to meet three members of the Llewellyn family at the Neath railway station and after talking to them and reading the information they had, it was soon clear that the focus of the search would be Cadoxton. There were references to Gellia Farm, Llan Gatwg Church and Cilffrew. The eldest member of the group was sixty-eight year old Ben Llewellyn, and he told me that their ancestor had emigrated to Canada in the early 1820s. The Llewellyn family had occupied Gellia in the 1820s.

Those facts about the dates, the name and Gellia gave me a chill. I took them to Gellia where Mr Brady, the current owner, was most obliging and showed them the old house, the small coal mine entrance and took them up the hill to see the views of the town and Swansea Bay. I walked with them down Cwmbach Road and into Cadoxton Churchyard (the church was locked so we failed to see inside, although they were keen to see it). They did stop alongside the Murder Stone and read every word and took several photographs and I had to take pictures of them with their hands on it. I didn't tell them the story and the possible connection.

But did I meet descendants of the family of Gellia, one of whose number was suspected of carrying out the murder of Margaret Williams?

Eight

MISCELLANEOUS HAUNTINGS

The Devil's Pathway

This story is located somewhere near the region of the Drummau Mountain. The story was passed on to David Rhys Phillips in the 1920s by George Smith of Neath Abbey.

The story goes thus: A farmer's girl making her way home to her farm near the mountain from Skewen late at night felt she was being followed by some ambling creature that ultimately caught up with her and walked by her side; she thought it resembled a calf.

When she arrived home she told her employer about it. He rushed out of the house after grabbing his gun and searched the immediate neighbourhood for the visitation.

He found nothing.

The next morning there were strange cloven hoofed footprints on the track leading to and from the farmhouse, which seemed to confirm the girl's story. Ever after the track has been called Llwybr y Cythraul, the Devil's Pathway.

Messengers of Death

Celtic folklore is clothed firmly in a belief of death messengers. In Ireland if one hears the gentle tap-tapping of a stick or something suchlike against the window

The Drummau Mountain which overlooks Neath.

at night, one is being warned that someone from that household is due to depart this life.

Another sign is the smell of sulphur. This is a nasty one, though, as it is thought to be the devil poking around in readiness to take someone to hell. The sound of dogs or hounds howling can happen in the daytime and at night, and is interpreted as the precursor of a death. The howling is uncanny and is still heard today, but whether calling the undead to eternity is another thing.

One house I knew of in Neath Abbey village was unnerving. From 1958 to 1973 whenever the dog, which didn't live there, was seen sitting by the front door the following day someone died and a few days later the coffin was carried out. This happened seven times. A wag in the Smiths' Arms came up with a solution. 'Shoot the dog.' Since 1973 no one in the house has passed away and the dog hasn't been seen either.

The eighteenth-century story of Modryb Ann from Melyn Cwrt in the Neath Valley, recorded by Marie Trevelyan in her *Folklore of Wales,* takes a different slant on the messengers of death. This one ultimately took Ann with him on a flying horse, but not before she had experienced a few trial runs.

In Marie Trevelyn's words:

At Mellincourt, about four miles from Neath, lived Modryb Ann, who on several occasions had been carried off by a main force over mountains and streams, through woods and glens, and returned again but would never let people know what her experience had been.

Rumours were current that a few times in her life she had been visited by a stranger – a grim figure in a long, grey cloak and a curious slouching grey hat. He had been seen, but his face was never visible, for the reason that people always observed him going to Modryb Ann's house and never coming from it. They also heard something like the clanking of keys or fetters, as the stranger moved along.

Modryb Ann's nephew came home from sea, and hoped while he remained ashore to solve the mystery of the stranger, if the latter paid a visit to his aunt.

One night in December his wish was gratified. He slept upstairs, and as there were wide cracks and small holes in the flooring, anybody could play the spy from there. In the dead of night, Jack, who was snoring, heard a knock at the cottage door. Modryb Ann, who slept on the ground floor, did not immediately hear the knock, which was repeated thrice. Then she got up and called out,

'Who's there?'

Somebody answered: 'You know who.'

Modryb Ann unbolted the door, and through the flooring Jack saw the grey-cloaked stranger entering, while his aunt sat down on the settle.

'I am come for you,' said the stranger.

'Sit a bit,' replied Ann, 'I am not quite ready. It's a cold night.' And she shivered.

Some talking went on, and presently the stranger threw his cloak off, revealing no more than a complete skeleton.

Jack shook with fear, and eagerly watched the couple.

'This is the third time of asking,' said the stranger, 'and tonight I come to claim my bride.'

Modryb Ann moved uneasily on the settle. There was more whispering between the pair, and presently the skeleton seized the old woman and compelled her to dance with him. Wildly they whirled, until Modryb Ann was giddy and begged permission to rest. While she did so, the skeleton resumed its cloak and hat, and prepared for departure. It threw the door wide open, snatched Modryb Ann under its arm, and when Jack went to the window to look out into the dim moonlight, he saw a grey horse waiting, upon which there was a bundle.

The skeleton, placing Ann in front, mounted the horse, and rode away like lightening. The people said Death had come for Modryb Ann, who was never seen again.

The Lure of the Water

The deep, wooded valley leading to the Melyn Cwrt Falls is certainly full of atmosphere. Above it all stands Melyn Cwrt Chapel, from which the track leading to the waterfall is not visible, not that the valley needs the help of a hillside graveyard to spook you. The dark ambiance does that alone. Is there a spirit, a ghost, calling people to the water for eternity? Another story captures the spirit in more ways that one, that of Mari Bensingrug. The lure of the river captivated Mari, and certain river-pools are reputed to lure people to suicide. D.R. Phillips carries the story thus:

> Of Mari Bensingrug, it was related that she was drawn by an unseen power to Cwm Sveirig, above the waterfall, some time after the middle of the last century [the 1750s]. On and on she travelled up the brook's side but something broke the spell and, and returning home, she complained that there was not enough water in the brook so had decided not to drown herself that day.
>
> Mari resisted the dark calling that day, yet it kept trying to fulfil its thirst for human companionship.

Another story in Philips' *The History of the Vale of Neath* tells of the 'case of an old lady who had abstained from food for many months but drank spring water every day. She would start of in the gloaming, but never reached the Nedd tributary towards which she directed her steps: the glamour of the woodlands through which she passed nailed her to a certain ultimate spot, and there she would remain for hours in all weathers.'

One asks if she, and others, are still waiting, longing for the brook to engulf them?

Flying Objects

There are many stories related to the Vale of Neath about flying 'things', from vampires, horses, fish, dogs and people who have been seen by others to levitate, or claim to have done so themselves. Such stories are connected to the times in which they were told.

Eminent people in the eighteenth and nineteenth centuries claimed to have seen fairies and other 'little people'; in the twenty-first century it is rare to find people believing in the evil, blood-lusting vampire, the corpse candle and the absolute prescription that death was calling soon, and the cortège procession with the coffin being carried by bearers of funerals long ago. They are beliefs and superstitions of their day; the modern equivalent that has people debating whether paranormal phenomenon is the 'flying saucer syndrome'. Like the sighting of ghosts, sightings of unidentified flying objects leave us with ambiguous feelings and thoughts.

One day science might give us the truth.

There are several sightings of UFOs in the Neath area, considering that the phenomena only hit our media in the late 1940s but has gained popularity and wide interest since then.

South West Wales saw a spate of recorded UFO sightings in the mid to late 1970s, centred particularly on Pembrokeshire and Carmarthenshire. Neath, too, had its share of 'visitations'.

A family, a brother and sister, living in Penshannel area of Neath Abbey in 1977 were standing in their front garden one clear evening when a bright light appeared in the north western sky. A bright star? They considered this and both their interest and curiosity had been aroused. They told me that the light seemed to drift down towards the Drummau Mountain just above the rock face where it hovered.

It stayed there quite still for many minutes and then to their astonishment they saw two figures or things coming out of the object, which still appeared like a bright, white light and again drifted down towards the ground. The figures came past the rock face and disappeared among the trees below.

The bright object remained in place, still and silent. After what seemed like ten minutes the figures reappeared and drifted back up to the 'craft'. They appeared to enter it and the object then began to move across the mountain, then upward and disappeared as though a switch had been thrown. The things just went out.

They said they had never believed in such things, had never seen anything like it and didn't wish to again.

Objects over the Valley

In 2002, Mike Davies, from Cadoxton was awoken by his dog late one night. He got up and from the kitchen window saw two bright lights in the north eastern sky over the Vale of Neath.

'I was intrigued,' he said, 'they looked too big to be planes and the two lights were flanked by two smaller, flashing ones.'

He got his video camera and recorded them for twenty minutes and then went to bed both exhausted and perplexed.

He decided to get in touch with an expert of unexplained sightings, Mr John Hanson, a retired police officer and the author of the book, *Haunted Skies*.

Mike had sent him a copy of the video; he was intrigued and presented the video evidence at a UFO conference in Truro, Cornwall.

Mr Hanson said, 'This is a very genuine piece of film of what looks like genuine phenomenon. It is clear that the size of the lights were two or three times larger than any aircraft. Similar formations of strange lights like this, normally triangular in shape, are nothing new to UFO organisations.'

He continued, saying that 'inexplicable light phenomenon like those seen and captured on film by Mike Davies excite the imagination, but one should be careful about forming snap judgements on matters such as these, because although it appears what he saw was very unlikely to have been orchestrated by human hands, one should not automatically believe that they are representative of any visitation by an extraterrestrial species. But there is some strange stuff out there.'

I have known Mike Davies for many years and he is the photographer who took the photographs for this volume and I have seen the film that recorded the sighting. It is strange; you can see the triangular shape of the objects and the two smaller flashing lights.

Unfortunately Mike said that after a few hours he gave up watching and went to bed. He regrets that, 'I should have waited until they disappeared of their own volition or indeed until daylight came.'

Craig-Y-Dinas

There are many legends about King Arthur and his sleeping knights related in Celtic lore, and the theme has parallels in several cultures throughout the world. The Vale of Neath has a well known Arthurian story; that the good king and his knights lay sleeping under Craig −Y-Dines in Pontneddfechan, awaiting the call to rise up and save Wales.

The story was first published by Elijah Waring, the Neath antiquarian, in his *Recollections of Edward Williams*, aka Iolo Morgannwg, and was used again in his *Handbook of the Vale of Neath*. Edward Williams had sent the manuscript to the Bristol poet Robert Southey, who in turn sent it to Waring to be used in his book.

Criag-Y-Dinas.

Before Southey resided in Keswick in the Lake District of England, he harboured an idea of living in the Cwm Nedd and spent time looking at Maes Gwyn near Pentreclwydau in 1801. His letters about the Neath Valley extol the virtues of the area, its scenery, language and traditions. Indeed his enthusiasm is boundless. He lodged with the Gronow family at Court Herbert House and Charles Gronow accompanied him to Maes Gwyn.

The idea of settling was doomed because Squire Williams' estate manager pointed out Southey's radical political views at that time and decided that he wanted no such left wing thought expounded in this area by one so eloquent as the poet.

Thus Southey left Neath for good, and Keswick became a centre for writers, rather than Neath. But he kept in contact with Waring and the legends of the valley would have been of great interest to him.

On receiving Iolo Morgannwg's story, Southey copied it to Waring and ever since publication has been one of the most loved legends in the area.

In 1925 David Rhys Phillips carried the story in his *History of the Vale of Neath*, a book that was reprinted in 1994 ensuring that this Arthurian legend lives on.

Considering that it is unlikely that the story wasn't known before Iolo's time it can be considered a tribute to his not inconsiderable imaginary powers.

Called the *Story of the Hazel Rod* we take the tale from D.R. Phillips:

A Welshman walking over London Bridge, with a neat hazel staff in his hand, was accosted by an Englishman, who asked him whence he came. 'I'm from my own country,' answered the Welshman, in a churlish tone. 'Do not take it amiss, my friend,' said the Englishman, 'if you only answer my questions, and take my advice, it will be of greater benefit to you than you imagine. That stick in your hand grew on a spot, under which are hid vast treasures of gold and silver; and if you remember the place, and can conduct me to it, I will put you in possession of those treasures'.

The Welshman soon understood that the stranger was what he called a cunning man, or conjuror, and for some time hesitated, not willing to go with him among devils, from whom this magician must have derived his knowledge; but he was at length persuaded to accompany him to Wales; and going to Craig-y-Dinas, the Welshman pointed out the spot whence he had cut the stick. It was from the stock or root of a large old hazel: this they dug up, and under it found a large, flat stone. This was found to have closed up the entrance into a very large cavern, down into which the both went. In the middle of the passage hung a bell, and the conjuror earnestly cautioned the Welshman not to touch it. They reached the lower part of the cave, which was very wide, and there saw many thousands of warriors lying down fast asleep in a large circle, their heads outwards, every one clad in bright armour with their swords, shields, and other weapons lying by them, ready to be laid hold of in an instant, whenever the bell should ring and awake them. All the arms were so highly polished and bright, that they illuminated the cavern, as with the light of ten thousand flames of fire. They saw amongst the warriors one greatly distinguished from the rest by his arms, shield, battle-axe, and a crown of gold set with the most precious stones, lying by his side.

In the midst of this circle of warriors they saw two very large heaps, one of gold, the other of silver. The magician told the Welshman that he might take as much as he could away of either the one or the other, but that he was not to take from both the heaps. The Welshman loaded himself with gold; the conjuror took none, saying that he did not want it, that gold was of no use but to those who wanted knowledge, and that his contempt of gold had enabled him to acquire that superior knowledge and wisdom which he possessed. On their way out, he cautioned the Welshman again not to touch the bell, but if unfortunately he should do so, it might be of the most fatal consequence to him, as one or more of the warriors would wake lift up his head, and ask if it was day. Should this happen, said the cunning man, you must without hesitation, answer, 'No, sleep thou on'; on hearing which he will again lay down his head and sleep. On their way up, however, the Welshman, overloaded with gold, was not able to pass by the bell without touching it – it rang – one of the warriors raised up his head and asked, 'Is it day?' 'No', answered the Welshman promptly, 'it is not, sleep thou on'.

So they got out of the cave, laid down the stone of its entrance, and replaced the hazel tree. The cunning man, before he parted from his companion, advised him to be economical in the use of his treasure; observing that he had, with prudence, enough for life, but that if by unforeseen accidents he should again be reduced to poverty, he might repair to the cave for more; repeating the caution, not to touch the bell if possible, but if he should, to give the proper answer, that it was not day, as promptly as possible. He also told him that the distinguished person they had seen was Arthur, and the others his warriors; and they lay there asleep with their arms ready at hand, for the dawn of the day when The Black Eagle and The Golden Eagle should go to war, the loud clamour of which would make the earth tremble so much that the bell would ring loudly, and the warriors awake, take up their arms and destroy all the enemies of the Cymry, who afterwards should repossess the Island of Britain, re-establish their own king and government at Caerlleon, and be governed with justice, and blessed with peace so long as the world endured.

The time came when the Welshman's treasure was all spent; he went to the cave, and as before overloaded himself. On his way out he touched the bell – it rang – a warrior lifted up his head, asking 'if it was day?' – but the Welshman, who had covetously overloaded himself, being quite out of breath with labouring under his burden, and withal struck with terror, was not able to give the necessary answer; whereupon some of the warriors got up, took the gold away and beat him dreadfully. They afterwards threw him out, and drew the stone after them over the mouth of the cave. The Welshman never recovered from the effects of that beating, but remained almost a cripple as long as he lived, and very poor.

He often returned with some of his friends to Craig-y-Dinas; but they could never afterwards find the spot, though they dug over, seemingly, every inch of the hill. He lived from a want of knowledge and prudence, teaching not to be covetous, not to neglect good advice, and never to trust that they can, without danger, give way to their own wishes, except one – the wish to be good.

Gitto Bach

Another legend, which refers to Gitto Bach of Rhos near Crynant, was collected and published in 1858 in the *Handbook of the Vale of Neath*. Gitto Bach's story was told by John Jones who died at Tyn-y-Graig in Crynant, aged ninety-one years in 1827.

The story goes thus:

Don't take to me, you silly young things—don't provoke an old man, now upwards of ninety years of age, by saying there were no fairies in Wales. If your great-grandfather was alive, he would confirm every word of what I say. 'Tis of what I saw, I speak, and will speak, while I have breath. I tell you that fairies were to be seen in the days of my youth by the thousand, and I have seen them myself a hundred times. Indeed, when I was a boy, it was dangerous to leave children in their cradles, without someone to watch them; so common was it for fairies to steal them away. There was poor Howell Meredydd Shone Morgan's family: what a trouble they had when they lived on the Rhos in the Creinant, when Gitto Bach was stolen away. Gitto was a fine boy, and would often ramble alone to the top of the mountain to look after his father's sheep; and when he returned he would show his brothers and sisters a number of pieces, the size of crowns, with letters stamped upon them, and resembling them exactly, only that they were made of a peculiarly white paper. When asked where he had found them he would say, 'The little children with whom I play on the mountain give them me'; he always called them the little children.

At length one day poor Gitto was missing. The whole neighbourhood was in a commotion. Search was made, but no little Gitto was heard of; two years elapsed, and still the desponding mother received no other intelligence, than in fresh cause of alarm for the safety of other children. For they had took to wandering on the mountains, and from one or two excursions they had returned with coins resembling those which had been given to Gitto previous to his disappearance; whereupon the family became doubly vigilant in watching these children, and the cottage door was cautiously secured with bars and bolts. One morning, as the mother opened the door, what should she see but little Gitto sitting on the threshold, with a bundle under his arm? He was they very same size, and apparently the same age, and dressed in the same little ragged dress, as on the day of his departure from the Rhos. 'My child.' said the astonished and delighted mother, 'where have you been this long, long while?' 'Mother', said Gitto, 'I have not been long away; it was but yesterday that I was with you. Look what pretty clothes I have in this bundle, given to me yesterday by the little children on the mountain, for dancing with them while they played on their harps'. The mother opened the bundle; it contained a dress of very white paper, without seam or sewing. She very prudently burnt it immediately, having ascertained that it was given him by the fairies.

Llewelyn Walter

Another sage, Dafydd Shon, who lived near Pontneddfechan in the late eighteenth to mid-nineteenth century, related the following:

About seventy years ago, there were two farmer's servants living at Llwyn-y-Ffynon; I knew them both well. They were returning from their work one fine evening at twilight and driving their little mountain ponies before them, weary with having toiled all day, carrying lime for their master's use. When they came down into a smooth plain, one of the men named Rhys ap Morgan, suddenly halted. 'Stop', said he to his companion, Llewelyn, 'do stop and listen to that enchanting music, that's a tune I have danced to a hundred times. I cannot resist it now. Go, follow the horses; I must find out the musicians and have my dance, and if I don't overtake you before you reach home, take the panniers off the horses. I'll be with you presently'.

'Music in such a spot', replied Llewelyn, 'in such a lonely place? What can you be dreaming of? I hear no music and how should you? Come now, no nonsense, come home with me'.

He might have saved himself this the trouble of this remonstrance, for away went Rhys ap Morgan leaving Llewelyn to pursue his homeward journey alone. He arrived safely, untacked the little horses, completed his day's work by despatching an ample supper and was retiring to rest without any anxiety about his companion, Rhys, who, he supposed, in his own mind, had made the music a pretence to go to the alehouse, which was five miles off. For, reasoned Llewelyn to himself, how could be the sound of music in that lonely spot, remote from any dwelling? The next morning when he found that Rhys was still missing, he reluctantly told their master that he must have assistance to attend the horses for that Rhys was not yet returned. This alarmed the farmer and his family, for Rhys was a very steady fellow, and had never before played the truant, although he was notoriously fond of dancing. Llewelyn was questioned and cross-examined as to where he had parted from him, and how, and why, and all about it. But to no one could he give what was considered to be a satisfactory answer. He said that music had allured him, and that he had left him to join the dancers. 'Did you hear the music?' inquired his master. Llewelyn replied that he had not; whereupon it was resolved that the alehouse should be searched. And that he should be sought for everywhere. But it was all to no purpose; no information was received of him; there had been no dance in the whole country round; not a sound of music had met the ear of anyone, and, in fact, not the slightest trace of the lost servant could be made out.

At length, after a strict but fruitless inquiry, suspicion fell on Llewelyn. It was supposed by some that he must have quarrelled with Rhys on their way home, and perhaps had murdered him. Llewelyn, thus accused, was taken up and confined on suspicion. He vehemently protested his innocence, although he could give no clear account of the affair; and things remained thus for a year, when a farmer in the neighbourhood, who had some experience in fairy customs, shrewdly suspected how the matter stood, and suggested that he and several others should accompany Llewelyn Walter to the very spot and at the very same time where he said he had parted from Rhys ap Morgan. This proposition was agreed to, and when they arrived at the spot, which was green as the mountain-ash, Llewelyn stopped. 'This is the very spot,' he said, 'and hush, I hear music; melodious harps I hear'.

We all listened, for I was one of them; but we heard nothing. 'Put your foot on mine, Davydd', said Llewelyn, whose foot was at that moment upon the outward edge of the fairy circle. I did so, and all the party did the same in succession, and we all instantly heard the sound of many harps in full concert, and saw within a circle of 20ft in diameter, countless numbers of little figures, the size of children of three or four years old, enjoying themselves vastly. They were going round and round the ring with hands joined. I did not perceive any varied figures in their dance; but as they were going round, we saw Rhys ap Morgan among them. Llewelyn at once seized hold of his smock frock, and twitched him out of the circle, taking great care himself not to overstep the edge of their ring; for once you are inside it, you lose all power over yourself, and become their property.

'Where are the horses? Where are the horses?' said Rhys impatiently. 'Where are the horses, indeed', said Llewelyn, 'where have you been? Come answer for yourself and account for your conduct. Clear my character, which your absence has cast the reproach of murder upon'.

'What stuff you talk, Llewelyn, go follow the horses, my good fellow, while I finish my dance, for I have not yet been above five minutes dancing. I have never enjoyed a dance like this. Oh, let me return to the dance.' said Rhys.

'Five minutes', repeated the enraged Llewelyn. 'You must explain the cause of your absence for this whole year. This foolish talk of yours about five minutes won't answer for me. So come, you must!'

He took him by main force. To all our questions he could say nothing, but that he had been absent from the horses five minutes, and that he was dancing very pleasantly, but of the people with whom he was he could give no account whatever; they are strangers to him, he said. He could answer no questions as to what he had eaten, or where he had slept, or who had clothed him; for he was in the same dress as when he disappeared, and he seemed in a very desponding way; he became sad, sullen and silent and soon took to his bed, when he died.

'And,' continued the narrator of the tale, 'the morning after we had found Rhys, we went to examine the scene of this extraordinary adventure, and we found the edge of the ring quite red, as if trodden down, and I could see the marks of little heels, the size of my thumb-nails'. He repeatedly compared the size of the heels to his thumb nail.

Old Danny

Greg Thomas was past eighty years of age when he related the following experience to me. Greg died in the early 1970s and had lived all his life in a cottage on the old turnpike road between Wernddu in Bryncoch and Alltwen.

A collier during his working days, his life seemed to have been punctuated by his work, his chapel, visiting the Gwyn Arms in Alltwen (he saw no conflict in frequenting a chapel and a public house). 'Convert them over a pint,' he would say with a grin. Hardly a day passed during his long life when he didn't walk home along the dark, narrow, hedge lined road that wound its way in the shadow of the Drummau Mountain.

Greg's story concerned a character known to everyone as Old Danny; indeed many didn't even know his surname. Old Danny was, it seemed, always leaning on the rickety gate outside his home, pipe in mouth, acknowledging everyone who passed by with a cheerful smile, usually shrouded in tobacco smoke, 'shw'mae gwas,' which was followed by a sideward-directed mouthful of spit. You knew that Danny was outside his house before you turned the bend in the road because you could smell the smoke.

It was on one of those delightful late July days, the warm, light evenings seemed to be never ending. Greg was earlier than was usual for him to be making his way home. It was a Friday evening; the Gwyn Arms had been quiet with most of the regulars away on a darts match. The hedgerows were filled with birds, rushed by nature nurturing their second batches of young. The occasional squirrel rushed across the road, the air was filled with the smell of cut grass. His thoughts strayed from the colliery, the minister in chapel gathering himself up towards his hwyl, and before he was within a hundred yards of Old Danny's cottage he could detect the welcoming odour of the smoke from his pipe.

And sure enough when he turned the bend there was Danny leaning on the gate. From a distance he acknowledged Greg with a wide grin and pipe in his hand.

'Nice night, gwas,' he said, followed by the usual spitting.

Greg stopped. 'Yes, nice bit of weather, Danny.'

They continued to talk for about ten minutes, Danny asking the same questions about people living in the area. He rarely left his home and would only see those who walked by. Thus his interest was always heightened by gossip.

'Time you fixed the old gate, Danny', said Greg as he prepared to leave. He noticed that with the old man's weight the gate leaned down and touched the ground but it always sprang up an inch or so allowing it to swing when the weight was removed.

Danny laughed. 'It doesn't bother me, and it's not likely to.'

With that Greg went on his way thinking Danny was as old as the mountain.

The following morning Greg was underground, working then in Tor-y-Graig Colliery, which was a drift mine that drove deep under the Drummau. Eating sandwiches during a break with his three butties, one of them said it was a pity about Old Danny.

Greg took little notice. One of the men asked, 'Why what's the matter with him?'

'He was found dead at the bottom of his garden yesterday dinner time by Prosser from the farm next door.' Greg asked him to repeat what he had said.

'It couldn't have been dinner time yesterday; I was taking to him past nine-thirty. I came away from the Gwyn early, well early for me, and I was talking to him, he was smoking outside his house.'

His colleague said he must have his days and times mixed up. 'No it was yesterday. He was found about midday. Prosser'll tell you. They shot his body off to the hospital in Neath. Post mortem, I suppose.' As they returned to their work his mate said, 'Ask Prosser.'

Greg said he did call with the farmer who confirmed that it certainly had been around midday that he found Old Danny slumped against a fencing post, he found him when he was walking in the field adjoining Danny's cottage. 'He was as dead as the Dead Sea,' he said.

He told the farmer that he had been talking to him in the evening. And the farmer said the same as his work mate. 'You couldn't have.'

'But I did,' implored Greg.

A few days later they walked along the road following Old Danny's coffin. 'I look back on that now after all these year,' Greg told me. 'I was really confused. I know I had spoken to him. I could smell that pipe smoke but there I still could smell it years after, particularly when I walked passed his house. Prosser is a very reliable man – I asked the undertaker and he said the same as Prosser, so did the doctor.

'Had the dead Old Danny waited to say s'long? And the gate, he had said its sagging wouldn't bother him.'

'I walked passed the house for years after because Old Danny died in the mid-1950s. Died? Or did he?' quizzed Greg.

The Cortege

Stories about ghostly funeral processions are common in Welsh folklore so it was with a degree of scepticism, although not expressed, that I responded to a call from William Walters, who lives in Ystradgynlais in the Swansea Valley. William is twenty-one years of age and spends much of his time in Crynant. He often walks home across Rhos Common, a lonely area of heath land, which is sparsely punctuated with small holdings.

It was during one of his journeys home along this dark road across the common when he found himself caught up in the haunting procession.

He started to tell me about it by saying he swore he hadn't been drinking. I take such experiences literally at face value; you soon learn when someone is making up a story by the inconsistencies that will become all too evident as the story starts to unwind:

I spend much of my time in Crynant my aunty lives there and so does my sometimes girlfriend. Often I sleep the night in my aunt's house but sometimes I walk home late at night. Of course, I have to cross Rhos Common. Normally I enjoy it, walking at night especially if the moon is out and the stars can be seen. I have never feared the dark. But since that night, I haven't walked it and will not again.

I was not far from the left hand turning that took me down Farteg Hill when quite suddenly I seemed to be surrounded by hundreds of these grey sorts of figures all walking in a silent procession. They, or it, was moving in the direction from which I'd come, Crynant. I was completely surrounded and something was forcing me to turn around and march with them. The figures were certainly ghostly because I could see right through some, which were hazy, others though appeared quite normal. Whatever, there were hundreds of them. I couldn't help myself, I seemed compelled to turn and walk with them.

This did happen although for some reason I can't recall turning around but I do remember the intense force I was trying to push against when I was going in the opposite direction. But I did turn, or was turned, because I was thrust and forced into walking with this procession.

I tried to clear my mind but I was sweating, although it was a cold night. The perspiration was clammy and was running down my face. As we started out on the long straight section of road across the common I could make out the figures and could see the outlines of a coffin and the six pallbearers. There hadn't been any sound at all but then I could hear the distinctive tramp, tramp, tramp, tramp of all those walking in complete unison. And then it stopped suddenly and one word was shouted, 'Change.' There was movement around me as six figures moved forward and replaced those carrying the coffin and seamlessly everything started walking again. Now I knew I was in a cortège, a ghostly cortège, a *canwyll corff*....

This 'Change' was called four more times, from where mind, I can't say, whether it was behind me or in front of me, the command just seemed to be uttered, before we reached the turning to Godre Rhos Chapel and its old graveyard. The tramping sound stopped as the cortège paused before crossing the brook into the graveyard. I heard the gate creaking and was still moving along with the figures. The moon glinted and caught the brass adornments on the coffin as it was carried to an open grave. With little ceremony it was lowered down and a preacher spoke in Welsh the traditional 'earth to earth', etc. With the exception of the word 'Change', this was the only other time I heard the sound of a voice. Except for the singing. Hauntingly and deeply the air was filled with the music of the hymn containing the words *O ffryniau Caersalem*. A hymn I knew well. It is often sung around the graveside. The last emotive verse goes like this:

O fryniau Caersalem ceir gweled
Holl daith yr anialwch I gyd;
Pryd hyn y daw troeon yr yrfa
Yn felys I lanw ein bryd;
Cawn edrych ar stormydd ac ofnau,

Ac angau dychrynllyd, a'r bedd,
Aninnau'n ddihangol o'u cyrraedd
Yn nofio mewn cariad a hedd.

I was still cold, clammy and with my breath coming in short bursts, which hurt my chest. I could hear the strains of the hymn echo across the common and it seemed to be absorbed into the mountain. And then suddenly it all stopped. The figures disappeared. I was alone. I stood there stunned. But within only a couple of seconds I ran from the graveyard and back to my aunty's house in the village. Luckily I have a key to the front door. I sat there, in the living room all night, terrified.

During daylight I went with William to Godre Rhos Chapel, as he refused my invitation to go there during the dark, and he described where he thought he had been standing but understandably couldn't be specific. There was no evidence of a grave having recently been filled in. But I did notice William's mood change.

Robert King in Llantwit Cemetery.

He became very uneasy and said he felt that he was being watched. He was much happier when I him drove home.

He was absolutely sincere and there were no contradictions in his story, which he related to me a few times during the few weeks since his experience. He said reflectively that he wished he had thought to drop something that he would later recognise. 'But there,' he added, 'I don't know what I was thinking properly.'

Godre Rhos Chapel has its origins in the early to mid-eighteenth century, and it is recorded that Howell Harris preached there. The current building dates from 1856. It is of particular interest to me because members of my maternal grandmother's family are buried there.

Stories like this are usually quoted as happening in the 1800s but William experienced this in the 1980s, so do the spectral funeral processions still move along our roads after dark?

Printed in Great Britain
by Amazon

55017230R00056